Journeys

PETER STERNS

Copyright © 2021 by Peter Sterns. 829520

All rights reserved. No part of this book may be reproduced or transmitted in any form or by any means, electronic or mechanical, including photocopying, recording, or by any information storage and retrieval system, without permission in writing from the copyright owner.

To order additional copies of this book, contact:
Xlibris
AU TFN: 1 800 844 927 (Toll Free inside Australia)
AU Local: 0283 108 187 (+61 2 8310 8187 from outside Australia)
www.xlibris.com.au
Orders@Xlibris.com.au

ISBN:	Softcover	978-1-6641-0513-3
	EBook	978-1-6641-0514-0

Print information available on the last page

Rev. date: 05/06/2021

Alzheimer's!

When into the mirror I look
Just who is it that I see?
Someone from a story book
Or is that someone really me?
I think at times I know this face
But mostly I wish that I knew
So I will just watch this space
For someone that I call – YOU!

Autumn

Summer's gone and autumn's come
And all the leaves will fall
It's like a half forgotten song
Whose words you can't recall
Winter winds are drawing near
But soon your heart will sing
For all the colors you hold dear
Will reappear again in spring!

Daybreak

Fog seems to cover the land like a shroud,
till the first ray of sunshine bursts through the cloud.
The forests that were so quiet and dark,
echo with the sounds of a song by a lark.

Flowers and berries, that quietly grew,
sparkle in the sun, heavy with dew.
Some people go to work, while others will pray,
this is the start of another lovely day.

Dues

The rush of silence to my brain
stops me from quietly going insane.
Songs of country music, especially Johnny Cash
stop me from doing something that's rash.

You can lie down and as at the sky you stare,
if He doesn't answer, doesn't mean He don't care.
It's true, that no matter how you strive,
you never manage to get off this world alive.

And as you lie there and think about your past,
the Good Lord has made His blessings last.
So think about it as you ponder the blues,
what did you do, to pay your dues?

End of a dream!

My heart it sings, sometimes it cries
My love has wings and than it flies
Than all my tears fall into the sea
And now I pray she'll return to me
But as time goes by, year by year
Gone is the love that I felt for her
I've lived on dreams that I can't forget
Once tears of joy are tears of regret
Now daylight comes with a golden gleam
Gone is my life, gone is my dream!

Hatred or love?

All this human suffering touches this heart of mine
As I would hope that it touches thine
No matter how we plead and pray to the Lord above
I believe that hatred has replaced the word of love!

Midnight on the homestead

Moonlight shines across the land
Distant hills can still be seen
Silvery sheds silently stand
Where once a town has been
Nothing there but barren ground
The town folks long since gone
No laughter here, not a sound
I wonder what went wrong.

Mountain range

Dark clouds in the sky above
I hear the rolling thunder
My grandson's eyes so full of love
I look at him and wonder
Will life to him be hard or kind
Will he have someone to love
We can plan, but we will find
It's in the hands of God above!

We are a rock!

The news we watch each day it is rather dire
Houses and lives are lost in a raging fire
A retired newsman and his wife, the only names I know
Both have lost their lives in the fire's mighty glow
Seven thousand people have lost all they ever knew
And it is said some fires were started by but a few
But we must go on and we must dry our eyes
We are a rock, we are an island, and an island never cries!

Little dreams!

Now there's a moon in the sky
Wish friends and your neighbours goodbye!
The moon and the distant old stars
They quietly shine from afar
The sandman he carries your dreams
Down on a silvery beam
Sleep now my darling, good night
Sleep in the star spangled light
Let dreams carry all your little cares away
Tomorrow is another lovely, lovely day
The moon and the distant old stars
They quietly shine from afar
The sandman carries your dreams
Way down on a silvery beam
So sleep now my darling, good night
Just sleep in the star spangled light
Let dreams carry you away
Tomorrow will be another day
Let dreams carry all your little cares away
Tomorrow is another lovely, lovely day.

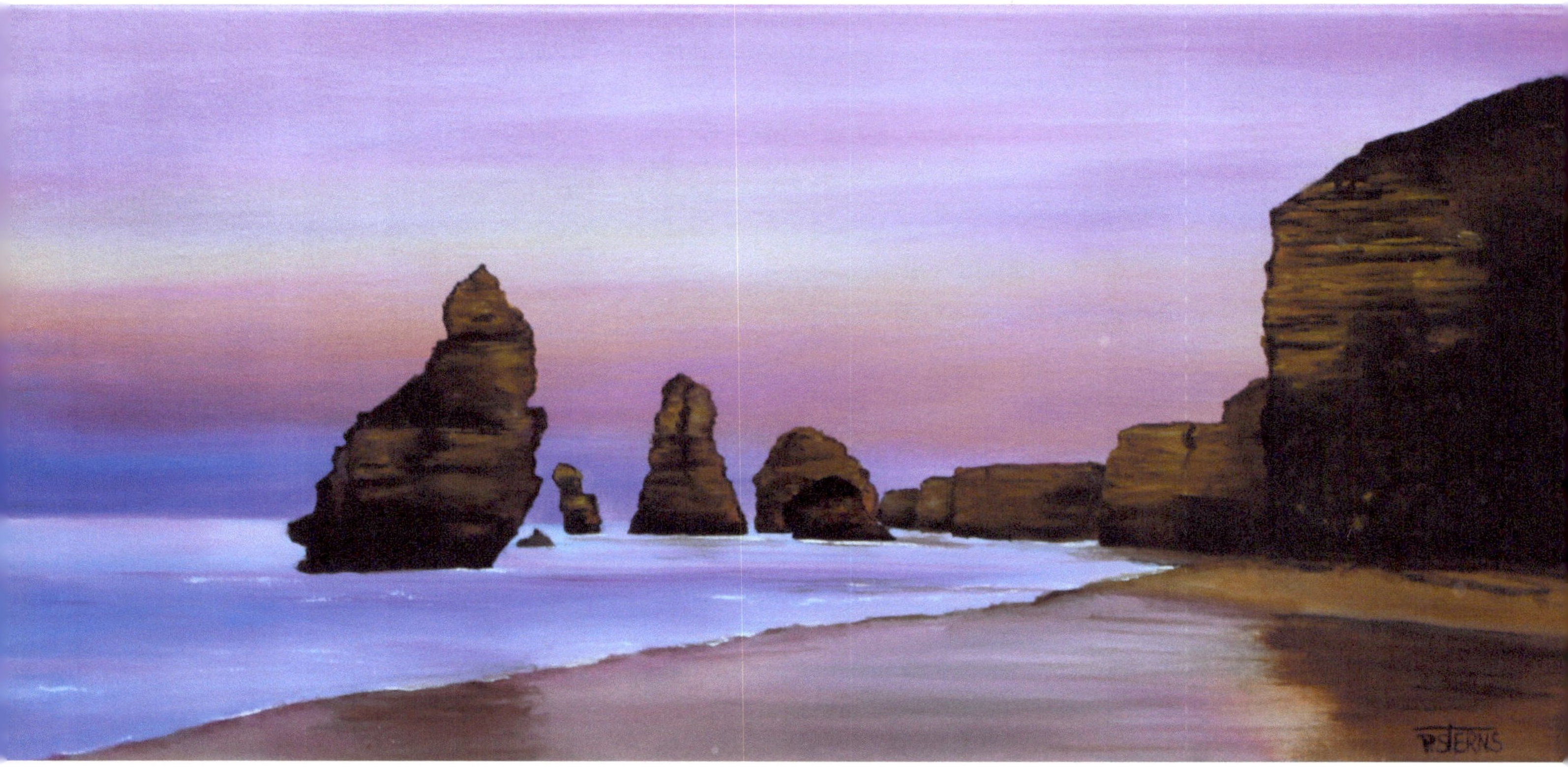
P.STERNS

About a man on death row

On golden wings!

For thirty years I sat and slowly waited
For the hanging man and for his rope
But now my soul it feels just so elated
As the Lord has given me so much hope
Even if the hangman comes tomorrow
In the morning sun around five
I'll end my life today without much sorrow
For God has promised me a brand new life
And as a child of six or maybe seven
I wanted to live my life just like a brave
But now at one and nearly sixty seven
I give thanks to God for what He gave
And I will give thanks today oh my Lord
For my heart today it truly sings
And in the sky I can see the eagle flying
As he soars along on golden wings
And I regret now the life I've taken
I'd like to atone for all my sins
For my soul now it has awakened
Once it flew around just like the wind.
And I give thanks today oh my Lord
For my heart today it truly sings
And in the sky I can see the eagle flying
As he soars along on golden wings
As he soars along up high on those
Golden, golden, golden wings.

A carol

Deck the halls for Jack and Molly
We almost reached another year
Let's forget our sins and folly
Have a steak and one more beer
It's the season for rejoicing
When we drink and have a bet
And our grievances we're voicing

Wishing we had Donald Trump instead
How can we face our future
If we don't have another plan
We can call it multi-culture
Well, good luck you foolish men
Yes gooood luck - you foolish men.

A child again

How are you? I said to him
I'm just fine, he said with a grin
He who used to be so wild
Said – I am as good as a child
I have soft and wobbly feet
And like a child I have no teeth
I can't run, it is not fair
Just like a child, I have no hair
There are some wrinkles on my brow
And like a child I need a nappy now
On simple things I rack my brain
Yes my friend, I'm like a child again.

A gift!

Are you a dollar short?
Perhaps even missed a date?
Remember a gift from the heart
Is never too late!

A lucky country

So how are you doing
And how do you fare
Is Banjo still writing
And why do I care
The country was burning
And the land was in flood
The water has been turning
The land into rivers of mud
Rivers where once was a street
Floating cars drifting along
I can hear a country beat
Wondering if it's a Slim Dusty song
If Banjo was writing his words
About Australia, about our land
Would it be about dying herds
About the country now turned to sand
It's still a sunburned country
That's there below our feet
But nothing like when the gentry
Landed here with the first fleet

A mystery of life

Oh, that kiss could have been much kinder
Said the commentator to the crowd
And I said that this must be a reminder
That he wasn't just thinking out loud
Now in the crowd there was a hush
It was followed by a pregnant pause
The man's cheeks turned pink as he blushed
When the crowd gave him applause
Just why this happens no-one knows
Sometimes I think life is such a joker
But they say that's how if often goes
In this great game, called snooker

A new beginning

Tell me oh tell me, sweet child of mine
Will you build me a temple or a towering shrine
Will you sing me praises and laud my name
Or will you cry and hang your head in shame
The days of old, of God and Jesus are gone
Now greed and ambition are worshipped as one
As if finding gold and oil on the South Pole
Is the only thing that could save our soul
The sands of time in the old hour glass
Are forgotten words that echo the past
Let us pray and learn to live and to cope
And let the New Year bring peace and new hope
And I really believe that now it is time
That a Muslim came and shook this hand of mine
When war and hatred and intolerance are gone
And all of mankind can finally live as one

A new dream!

These aren't teardrops on my pillow
They're just moonbeams from the sky
I am not a weeping willow
It's just day dreams passing by
They are not a sign of sorrow
Nor a heart that's on the run
For I know that by tomorrow
This old heart ache will be gone
Gone will be all this dreaming
Of a love that might have been
For my heart will now be singing
With the new days golden sheen!

A new love

I don't hurt as much as I used to
And I only cry once in a while
But the teardrops I did cry for you
Surely could have filled the Nile
If old Moses was here, he would say
Oh the trouble you've caused me
Because I have tried and tried all day
But I just cannot part the Sea
And if I should have to live forever
I guess you would always be unkind
But I'm not afraid to pay the devil
To keep your memory from my mind
So now the last teardrop it has fallen
And I'm no longer filled with tears
I have a new love that is calling
And she will always be right here.

A prayer!

I'm just a writer of simple words
And I know how helplessness hurts
For all the things that cause me pain
In drought, fire and falling rain,
Is the knowledge that in this life
I can't help to ease the pain of my wife!
So Lord, I ask for her sake
Teach me to take,
And I ask not for mine,
How to take one day at a time.

A soldier's grave

I am sure I saw the ghost
Of a fellow soldier passing by
As I listen to the last post
The sadness of this makes me cry
The futility of another war
Raging since the start of time
Is leaving yet another scar
On this aching heart of mine
And as I stare upon this grave
I wonder as the years go by
Will anyone know they were brave
And remember just the reason why
Who cries for us, Lord of all
Now that our life is gone
Lying here in a six foot hole
A blanket now a block of stone

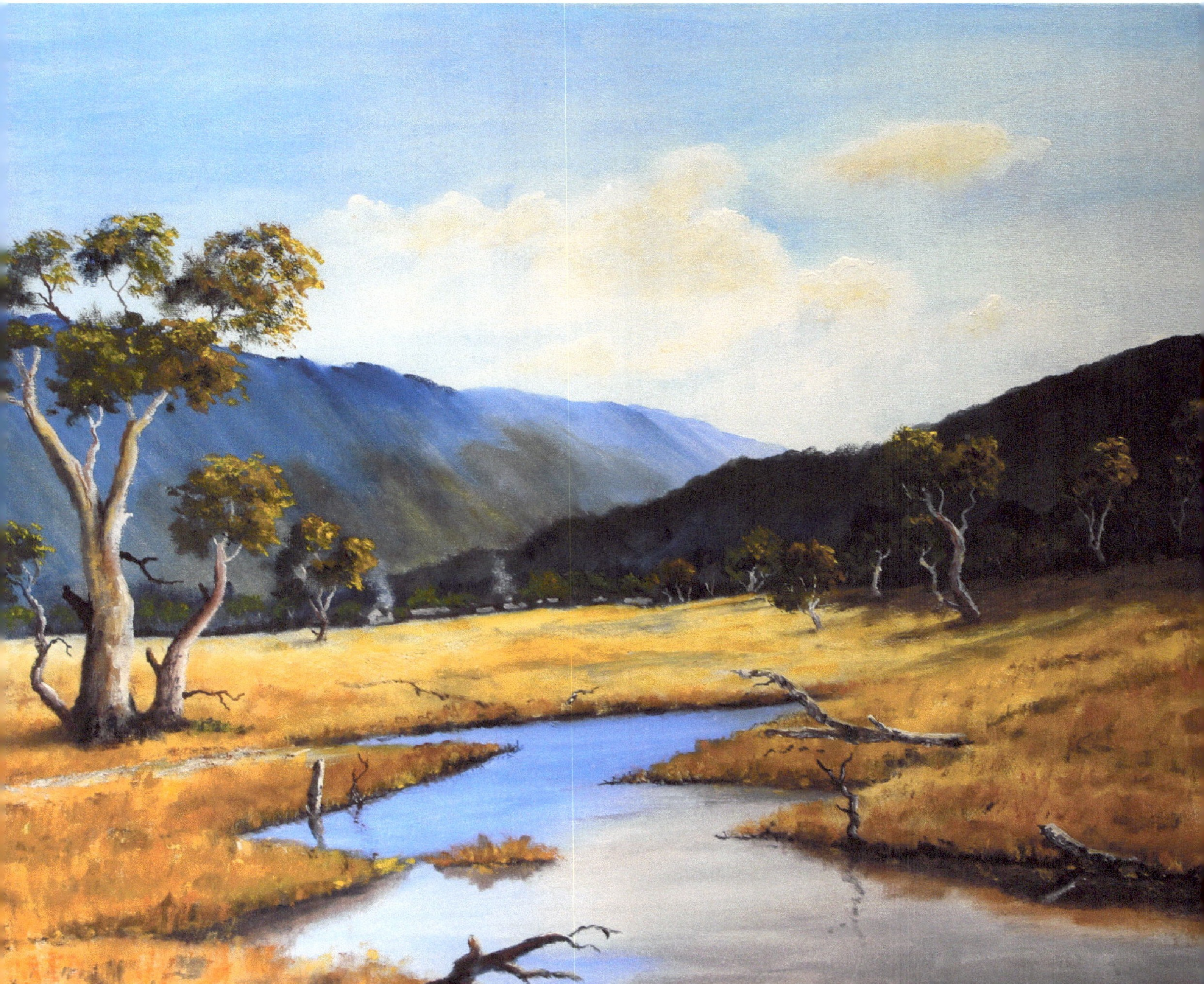

A warrior's soul

Tell me now, oh lord of war
What is the reason that I fight
No-one here is keeping score
And when will we see the light
The Romans once called you Mars
Fought with shield and spear
The modern warlord drives a car
And Armani suits will wear
Many a mother is bound to cry
While her son dies, trying to be brave
His final thought, why must I die
And sleep in a lonesome grave

Abandoned farm

The sun is setting, runs for cover
The world's in a wondrous glow
There under the trees I soon discover
Houses stand, three in a row
Fences down, timbers rotten
No horses tied to a wooden beam
In ten years it'll be forgotten
Another lonely settler's dream.

My father-in-law, the sailor.

Father Abraham

When I was a young sailor
as a Dutchman I was born,
a Harbourmaster, not a tailor
who sailed around the Horn.

If my stories caused duress,
they were just me, were my own,
and I hope you think of me no less,
now that I am gone.

And should I die before you, darling
and go to the Lord up above,
via con dios, my darling,
via con dios, my love.

My wife, my children and their kids,
I know I didn't always do enough,
think of me and smile a bit
as I held you in my heart with love.

Accuracy!

A wharfie who had his 45th birthday to celebrate
Decided to call in sick rather then turn up a day late.
So after his friends did all their birthday wishing
He took his boat out on the sea for a spot of fishing.

As luck would have it while out there on the sound
A wave struck the boat and he promptly drowned.
Now drifting up to Heaven and pondering about his fate
He was met by Saint Peter waiting at the Pearly Gate.

Who said – I'm here to welcome you and take you into the fold
It isn't every day we get someone who is a couple of hundred years old!
You got that wrong, the wharfie said, I only just now turned 45!
Not so, was the reply for according to your timesheets, you're 205!

News flash. Trainers and sportsmen caught with illegal drugs. Performance enhancing – what a sport.

Accusations

Like a chicken sitting on a roost
we are starting to feel the strain,
when we are of foul play accused
about our methods and how we train.

The hormones you mistakenly found
were from a doctor, for legitimate use,
we are standing here on solid ground,
they were not for any sporting abuse.

It would seem we should feel guilt
when our trainers are treated like thugs,
if our swimmers like wrestlers are build,
it's because of hard work, not due to drugs.

Addiction!

Voices I am hearing, voices that seem so real
Pain that I imagine, is agony I feel
I say – dad, please help me for I don't want to die
All my senses are reeling; the whole world seems to cry
Mary Jane so sweet, the future one big hole
Soon I will be dead, Lord have mercy on my soul!

Old age!

When I was 16 I could have peed
Over a fence that was six feet.
But now at 82 I found
That with both feet on the ground
The best I can do is gravity feed!

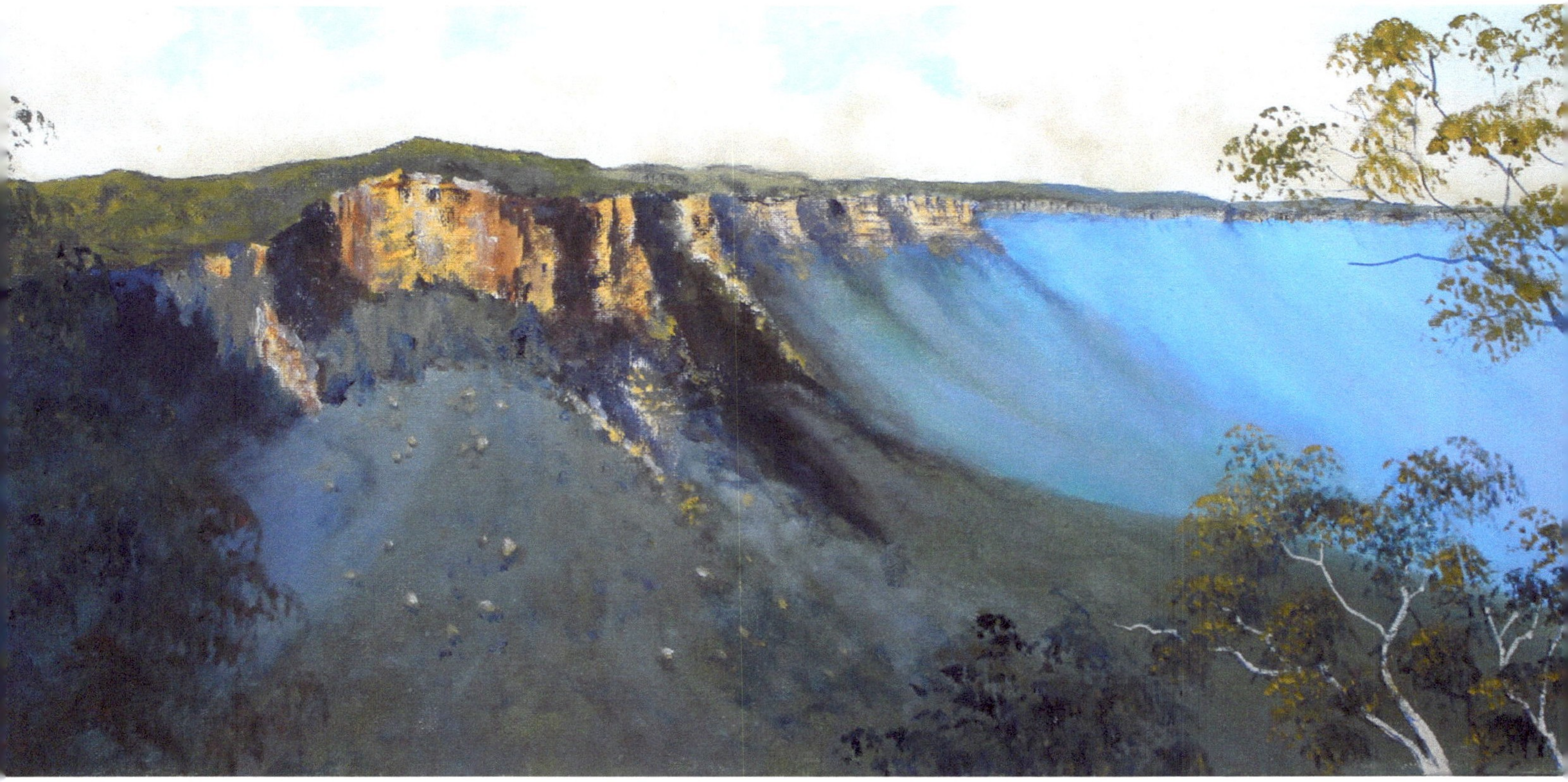

Aging

The older I get, the less I fret
About just what is ahead
At times I think out loud
Life and what it is all about
The choices we made
Pass like a parade
With the friends that I have
And the love they gave
The friendships of the past
And how long they did last
The older I get, the less I forget
Friendships with no regret

Almost done

As time passes the mind wanders back
Along a life that was a one-way track
I can't tell anymore what is real
But I guess that's just how I feel.
I can't help what I am feeling
Because at times I think I'm dreaming.
Bury me in the cold, cold ground
Where the blue gums sing in the wind
So I can close my old weary eyes
And kiss this lonely world goodbye.
I know it is getting late
I can see the ghosts of my dreams fade.

Alone

Who am I and where are you, love of mine
Questions that haunt me with words unsaid
But to be sure just one question at a time
I follow the trail with feet made of lead
It tends to disappear up there in the clouds
There's never a hint, not even a token
So much silence, nothing ever said out loud
Just millions of words, none of them spoken
The sun shines bright up there in the sky
The dew drops on the grass, they glisten
I can speak of love till the day that I die
But there's no one left for me to listen

Alzheimer's

One gets old and one forgets
No more pain and no regrets
Kids grew up and they grew tall
Perhaps this isn't so bad after all
Who are you and just who am I
Another birthday, maybe I'll die
Who really cares, who is to know
A year has gone, how many to go
But who will know me, who will care
When I just sit here, smile and stare
Memory and self are gone, are lost
I'm living still, but I'm just a ghost

Ancient history

Where are the temples of love that were build
Are they gone with the ravages of time
Can't ever find the ruins of guilt
No remnants of love I could find
Pyramids are reminders of powerful men
The Sphinx stands alone without a word
Sandstorms howl and whisper now and then
And sometimes the cry of a soul can be heard
They have written about queens and kings
Of kingdoms so great and some small
And sometimes relics are the only things
That remind us, we're not that tall
They speak of love, the greatest there was
Every generation keeps saying the same
And they are fighting for whatever cause
Leaving ruins in the dust without even a name
So where are the temples, build for the Gods
The ones they worshipped, to whom they would pray
Nothing to find but a few written words
And soon they too will be gone by the way

Inspired from a song by Isla Grant.

ANZAC Ghosts

As you march to the sound of the last post
Are you back there and are you seeing a ghost?
The ghosts of mates from those years gone by
Do you wish that they never had to die?

Can you hear them marching proudly through your mind?
Can you feel them as you can the passing wind?
Do you wish for a handshake or for a mate's embrace?
For no matter what, you can't forget their face!

Don't be too proud to show your feelings or shed a tear
They died for your freedom and did it without fear.
So can you hear them, can you feel them?
Because I know, you will never forget them!

Apathy

"I've got it good, I'm no jerk,"
He says as he defiantly at you stares.
"Why should I go and look for work?"
Well, apathy is a problem, but who cares!!!

Ashes of love

I'm looking at you and though you are here
I'm all alone
Time stands still, the years they moved on
I'm all alone
How can it be, where did it go
Where is the love
Dreams in the night, forgotten by day
Where is the love
Plans for tomorrow, plans for forever
Shattered like glass
Sunshine one day, then stormy weather
Dewdrops glisten on grass
Where does it go when the love dies
Is it ashes of love
Teardrops in clouds and stormy skies
A lifetime of ashes of love.

At the forest pool!

Serenely the water flows
While I wait for the night to be
There is peace as the sunlight glows
I hear birds singing in the tree.

Here in the fading light
My thoughts they are far away
Soon the moon will brighten the night
The end of another lovely day!

After seeing a documentary on Auschwitz.

Auschwitz

This is a monument so dark and cold
A monument to a million tortured souls
To remind us all, to live like friends
To forgive each other, to make amends.
I want to go, but I cannot leave
I did not know them and yet I grieve.
The sun shines warm, I feel so cold
I cannot leave, who's got me hold?
A million faces, there in my mind
Not a single soul here I could find.
I hear the echoes in the empty halls,
The sound of pain, as someone falls.
Millions suffered here and died
The clouds above from the tears they cried.
My Lord, how did this come to be?
Weren't your children meant to be free?
Sixty years have come and gone,
Yet people die, can't live as one.
Will our children learn from our past?
Or is the cycle meant to last?

Australia Day!

In years gone by they came here at the king's pleasure
But now we recall those times drinking beer at our leisure.
The worst we feel that could happen is when we watch the Tellie
And we see a film about such legends as Ned Kelly.

They thought it was the land of milk and honey
The streets were paved with gold, the walls lined with money.
But the truth is it's the land of sunburned fields and plains
At times ravaged by fire, at times drowned by flooding rains.

Some think they still hear the thunder of Pharr Lap's famous hooves
When it's only the drum of the rain that is lashing at our roofs.
And where years ago the bullocks pulled their heavy loads
We now have railway tracks and four lane bitumen roads.

But there are some people who still don't understand
That we are one people who come from many a land.
And it makes no difference if you're well off or work for your pay
We all know that January 26 is always Australia day.

Autumn of life

I am angry at the world
And I'm angry every day
A can laze and I can toil
I can waste my hard earned pay
What happened to the dreams so bright
Bright as the midday sun
Do they just fade at night
Before they have ever begun
Now that life is running out
Yes it's running out of time
I realise what life is all about
But I'll be leaving it all behind
The questions of life, my destiny
Are there in memories I recall
And the answers are up to me
As autumn leaves have stopped to fall

Autumn.

An acorn falls out of a tree,
it hits the ground, but first hits me.
It gives me such a fearful fright –
Who threw this and then ducked out of sight?

Boy, oh boy, a little shock, I must confess,
but a little shock does not cause stress.
You see when autumn comes around
the acorns tend to fall to the ground.

This is nature at its best,
preparing for winter, to rest.
So if you look up, the sky to see,
do not stand under an old oak tree.

Awards

Who should get a Nobel Prize
Surely not for telling lies
Nor has the criteria been met
For shooting 50 people dead
Or perhaps for standing tall
Building a retaining wall
That deserves a resounding thump
For non-other but Donald Trump

The baby.

Oh, come on this is not trick,
touch my tummy and feel it kick.
We don't know if it's a girl or a boy,
but it's going to be a bundle of joy!

Be happy!

It doesn't seem all that funny
When you see it from my point of view
Despite of all your position and money
All that you have is not really you
But you don't want to know about it
You say, you've heard it all before
Your lifestyle is so over crowded
And your wife is the one who keeps score
Well, you just might think I'm crazy
Or that I am so far out of touch
I'm neither bored nor am I lazy
But money doesn't mean all that much
I remember the words of my old pappy
That too much work was the original crime
Just learn to live and to be happy
Before you all have run out of time!

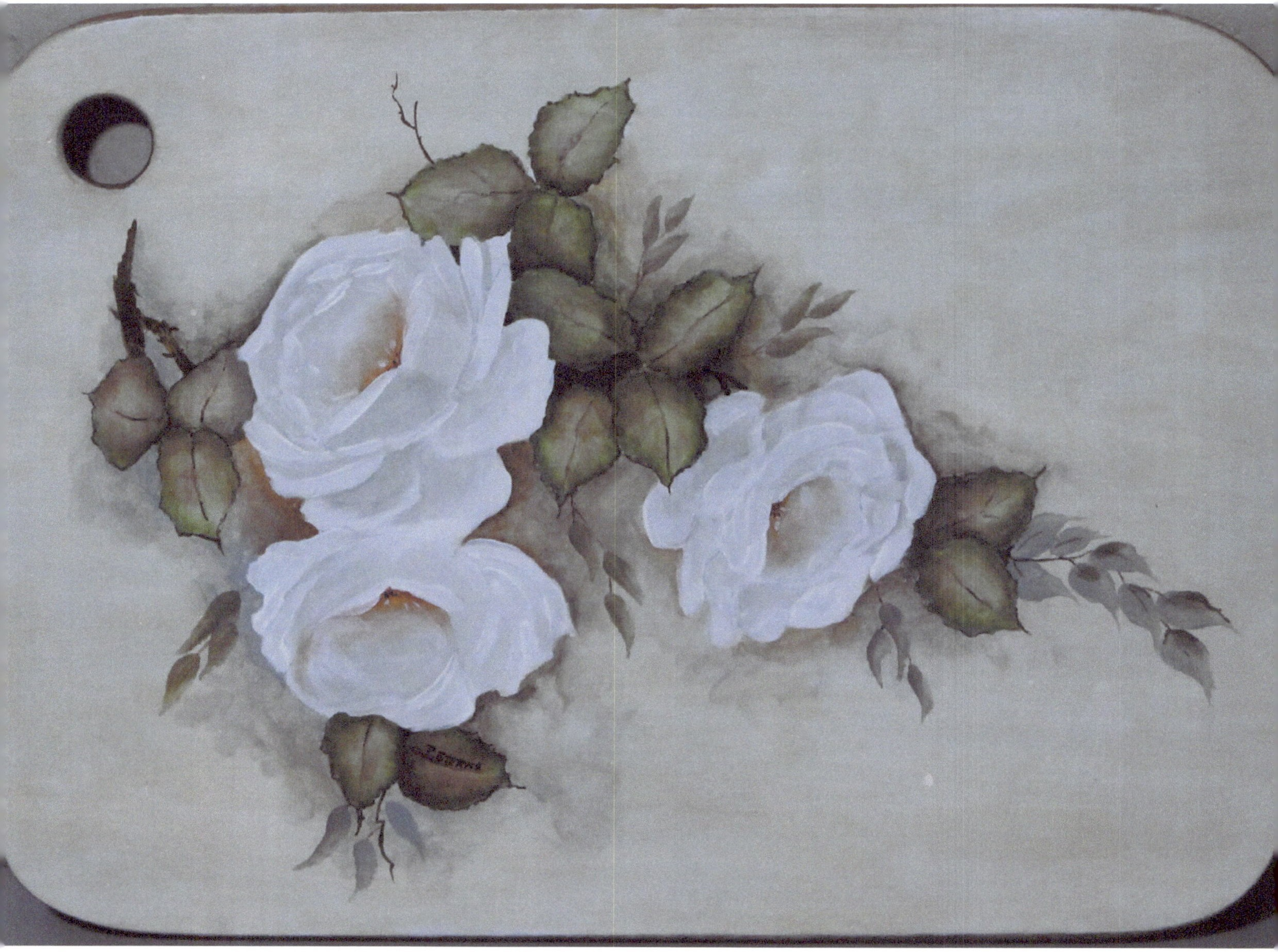

Big bang theory

Mention not my foolish pride
Lest my ego I must hide
Which is there for all to see
For I am mightier than thee

Birds

Cockies, I'm told, are one of a kind
Like cheese that is mouldy or has no rind
They screech and squawk in their own style
And can be heard for well over a mile
I have a neighbour with a cocky that talks
Who tells everyone that she has big nawks
What that really is, I'm not quite sure
But I do hope that one day they'll find a cure

Blessings

If the Lord had my soul
In the palm of His hand
Would I cry or would I laugh
I guess what more could I ask
For that blessing would be enough!

Borrowed words

But when the autumn of your life has come
You see that life has been easy, but for some
Who find the nights are cold and lonely
When they think of their one and only.

You remember the smile on your face
When you felt the love in her embrace,
And if at times you were unwise,
It's now too late to apologise.

But until I too step onto that golden shore
When I will have to weep no more,
And I find that peace in the valley for me,
Please show my heart some sympathy.

Bygone days

Have you ever thought that the wind
might be the gentle touch of a love lost,
the tender caress of your mother,
the brisk embrace of your father?
If you haven't – than go outside,
close your eyes,
and let him hug you!
Let the murmur of the breeze
tell you of the times gone by,
remind you of your childhood.
Dwell on the good things
and the good times to come.
The wind is your friend.

Written today, but thought of long, long ago.

Carers

You never know if one day you'll need help
Be it to do shopping, changing nappies or eating kelp.
This is something we all one day might face
And if it happens, it is not a disgrace.
It is all a dreaded part of just growing old
And to those who are blessed with hearts of gold,
Who do their work with smiles, not with curses
Those doctors, sisters, carers and nurses,
And it is that often to our own regret
These people to give our thanks we forget.
So on behalf of all those whose health is failing
A heartfelt thanks to the carers from the ailing.

Changing seasons

When I was young and oh so free
I wanted to see a ghost
Because the thing you cannot see
Is what you desire the most
Butterflies and strawberries
Are memories of the past
And just like all our stories
Some will fade and some will last
But the more you try
You find the harder it is
And as time goes by
The more detail you will miss
So be grateful for what you recall
Because it is all there is
Summer, winter, spring and fall
Are like the memory of a kiss
Forever it will linger on
And seem sweeter as you age
But when the book of life is done
It's the last words on its page.

Charlie's shoes

Seems like just the other day
When Charlie had the blues
And I heard someone say
Walk a mile in Charlie's shoes
Now it's 14 years later
And so many miles down the track
Charlie's feeling so much better
But I can't find my way back
All that I can say
Is if someone's got the blues
Turn and walk the other way
Let them walk in their own shoes

Cheers!

I don't know what fate awaits me
There's no use to sit and cry
You cannot just get religion
On the day you up and die
There are 16 vestal virgins
Waiting there to take me home
And some 27 drunken sailors
Telling me that I am wrong
Softly, softly little darling
Say a prayer lest I forget
Ever loving, ever caring
In a life that's full of regret
I lift my glass in salutation
To the ones that passed away
And give thanks to the generation
That has lived another day
So let us drink to a new direction
Let's continue in our dream
Where we thought all is perfection
In a life that might have been!

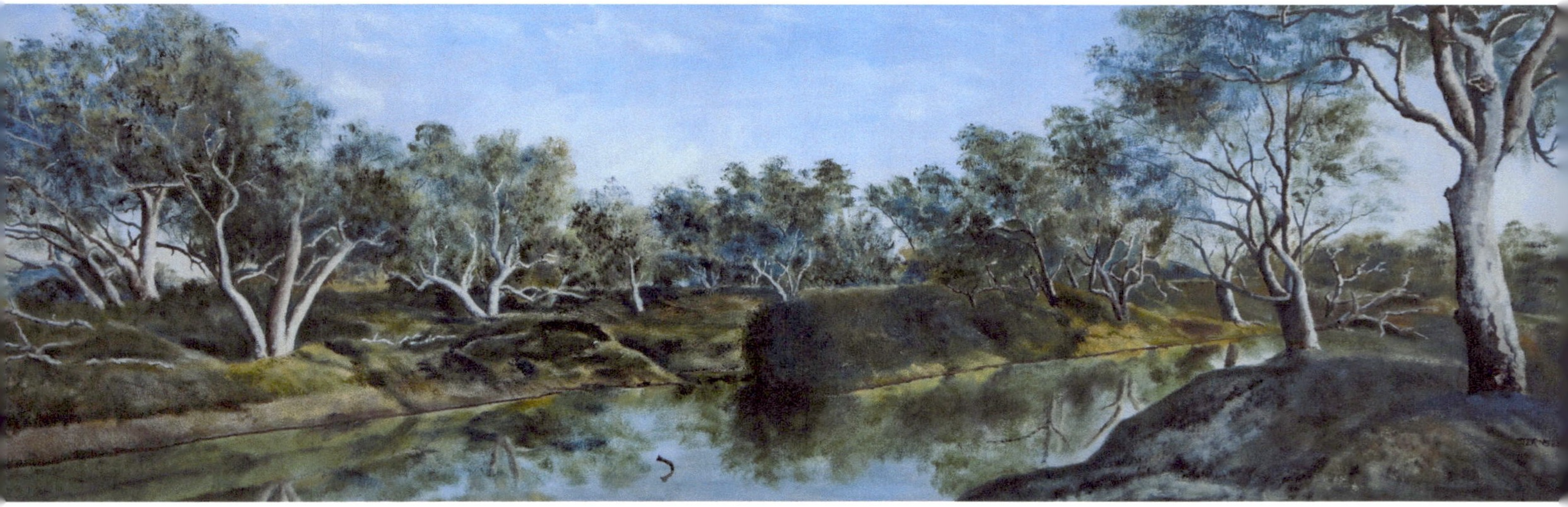

Childhood blues!

The world of a child seems so different
Everything is so shiny and new
But if you think seeing is believing
It can turn out to be so sad and blue
For one evening when I was out walking
I heard this strange little sound
I saw my father kiss a young maiden
And my whole world turned upside down
I never quite had the courage
To ask about what he had done
But I always heard father saying
That mother was his only one
Years later I saw them kissing again
And suddenly I knew it was true
For mother you were that young maiden
And father is still kissing you!

Childhood dreams

How I miss those lovely nights
When I had those childhood dreams
Pink elephants in graceful flight
And trains that were driven still by steam
Dragonflies hovering above the water
An eagle gliding through the sky
Golden hair on the neighbor's daughter
A smile in her pretty blue eyes
Fresh bread slices on the table
And straw mats on the floor
Horses and cows in the stable
A sprig of green leaves on the door
St Nicholas at Christmas time
The Easter bunny in the spring
Songs we sang with words that rhyme
And a choir that could sing
Yet I know the bunny never has spoken
And Father Christmas is not real
Our parents give us this token
Of how children should really feel
Where are they now those childhood days
And those dreams of so long ago
I guess they've gone their separate ways
And melted away just like the snow!

Choose

It is life's greatest contradiction
That its love that makes us whole
But I've come to this conviction
That it can also burn your soul
It can be tender or it can be mean
This whole blessed life it is a big show
Which it is, remains to be seen
But you just need to give it a go

Christmas 2018

Christmas time speaks of a new tomorrow
The birth of Gods son from above
It gives hope and takes away all sorrow
Most of all it gives the world His love
It gives us joy and great exaltations
We treasure it each and every year
In His word we will find salvation
Even if our life's end cometh near
This time of year is for celebrations
Reflecting on what for us He's done
The wish for all of our nations
Peace on earth for each and every one.

Christmas wish

On the eve of great elation
Let us pray instead of fight
And may the Lord of all creation
Be your ever guiding light

Circle of life

We are born screaming and crying
Yet our parents they smile with glee
Mother said it was almost like dying
Father thought – how can that be
You grow up and go to college
You last 8 weeks and one day
Never found the tree of knowledge
But you hope to find your way
There is work, a woman and children
And something that they call love
Yet the yearning inside you is building
Because somehow it's never enough
There are words in my memory
So familiar they all sound
They speak of our destiny
Of a grave there in the ground
Always talk to and trust the Lord
My father's words so distant now and faint
Remember son, you have been told
When you die, you're not a Saint
So when it's time to leave this earth
It is a blessing joined with pain
That started long ago with your birth
And shows the circle is complete again.

Closer every day

As the hand of time the midnight nears
Are we running out of chips
Are we gripped by our primal fears
By the nearing of the apocalypse
We are ravaged first by drought
The lamenting can be heard
Then fires we have fought
Now rain drowns out the words
Storms are lashing foreign lands
And a pandemic sweeps the world
No use crying and wringing our hands
If the Lord has the last word

Clouds

Now I'm old it is clouds I see
That dance to life's symphony
Don't know how they get it right
Dancing all day and night
Sometimes they just up and fly
Leaving nothing but a clear blue sky
On other days, as if in pain
Their teardrops fall just like rain
But if they're angry and you dislike
You can see a mighty lightning strike
And when all arrows have been hurled
A rainbow greets a brand new world

Colours

Grandma loves you and now you love me
Grandpa, what colour is the sea?
My hair is blonde; my eyes are blue,
You love me and I love you.
The sky is blue, the grass is green
But snow is something I haven't seen.
I know the sun up there it is bright
And you tell me that snow is white.
I learned I shouldn't fight
I hear things like, I hope you're right.
And that with life we learn to cope,
But tell me please, what colour is hope?
Well young man, when all seems lost,
Hope is something we keep at all cost.
But if you lose it and can't get it back,
Than I guess that hope is black.
Hope is anything, you see
Any colour you want it to be.
Just like a rainbow up above
But mostly hope is the colour of love.

Coming home

Christmas spirit everywhere
Another year is almost gone
There is so little time to spare
My earthly work is nearly done
All those memories in my head
So much love still in my heart
I wish that I could stay instead
Yet pretty soon I know we'll part
It might not be today or tomorrow
But I can see the setting sun
Think of me but not with sorrow
Please tell the Lord I'm coming home!

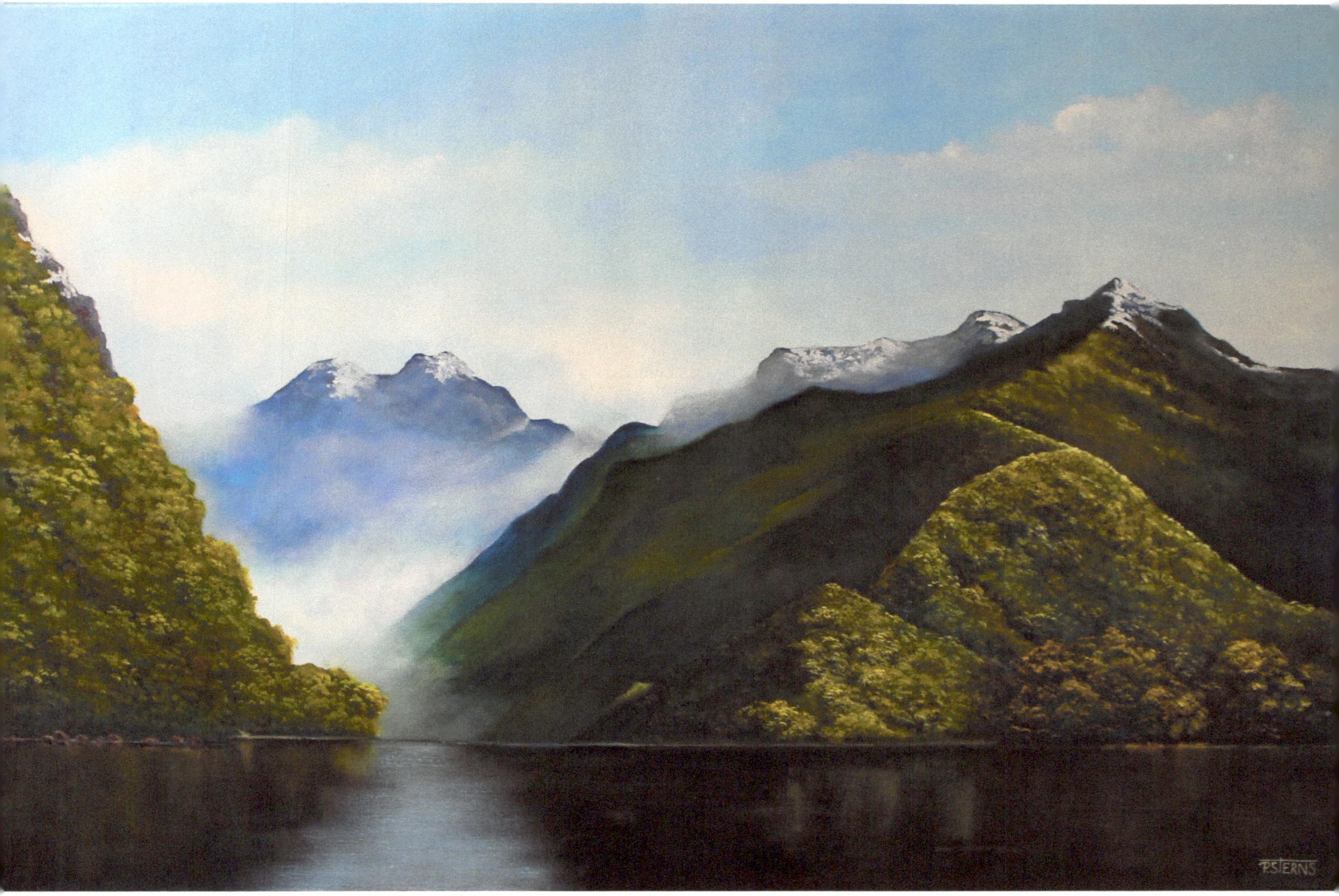
P.STERNS

The conflicts of the mind

The memories of the long forgotten kind
are found in the darkest corners of our mind.
The pain in our heart we try to disguise
with what others see, as fire in our eyes.
The pain of long ago, of childhood days
seems to linger like a red hot haze.
You can't decide whether to hate or forgive,
at times you want to die, yet you want to live.
You want to be you, to share with mankind,
yet you are unable to leave the past behind.
You know you cannot do as you wish or please,
you need to walk the path of the Lord, of peace.
A book you are writing of days gone by,
in the Bible you read about an eye for an eye.
The hate you feel is strong, and yet you find
that hatred is not going to ease your mind.
And as you pray to God and except His gift,
you feel the awesome burden slowly to lift.
As your faith grows and becomes strong,
you realise the things of the past were wrong.
But they are behind you, finally gone
and life itself, at last can go on.
The sun again shines and keeps you warm,
the Lord's love protecting you from harm.
As you learn your own boat to steer,
the path ahead is bright and clear.
You are grateful for the chance at a new start
as you sing in praise – How great Thou art!

Confused

There is something in the back of my mind
But is it ahead of me or far, far behind
They say it's a disease that has no cure
Yesterday I had my doubts; today I'm not so sure
I'm trying to see what this is all about
Then it happened, I started to think out loud
And as it came to me, like, right at the end
I said – keep looking for the truth, it is out there my friend

Confused

At times I get crazy
Confused, even blue
The world appears hazy
And nothing is new
The memories they come
And some of them fade
At times I am at home
Or perhaps on a date
But I cannot tell you
If the world turns around
There are people I talk to
But I don't hear a sound
Don't know if I'm screaming
If this is Heaven or Hell
Don't know if I'm dreaming
In my own padded cell

Coping with life

I look at the obscenity
Loosely called humanity
Those that will those that don't
Others still that simply won't
Tell me mate, what's your excuse
For being wild, for drug abuse
Always someone else's crime
Yet you're the one that's doing time
Now you say you had it rough
Life was hard and not a laugh
Fought a lot but couldn't win
Well, hard luck – learn how to swim

Coping

They say, give it time, just give it time
Perhaps one day, the sun again will shine
But until then, turn on the lights
Stars alone, don't shine so bright
How long before again I'll sing
And just how long is a piece of string
So give it time, just give it time
Is just a lame and useless line

Counting blessings!

In this life we keep on guessing
At what is real or might have been
And when we count our blessings
It is never quite the same
We have gifts that we've been given
Yet we don't share with anyone
We just keep right on living
As we think we're number one
And it never seems enough
For we worship gold and banks
You should turn to the one above
And to Him give words of thanks.

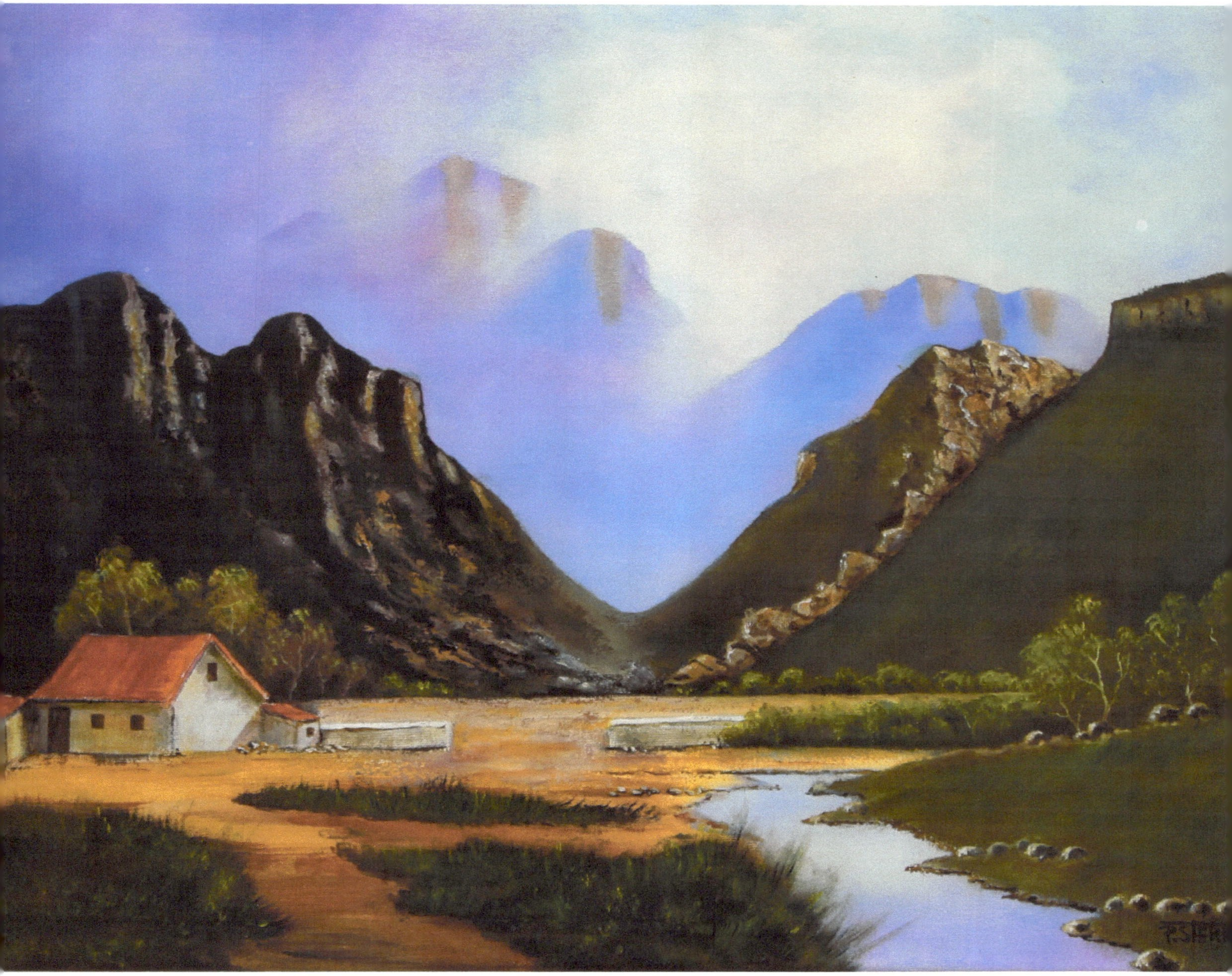

A man burns his estranged family to death

Crime of passion or obsession

Love is just a game of chance
But be that as it may
Worldwide it is called romance
And it's played out every day
It starts off with – I love you
With nights of passion and lust
But when those moments are through
The words of love turn to dust
Men who their love will profess
Beat their wife just to be sure
It is love they say, they confess
Single minded and so pure
But when you burn your family
Your children and you wife
It is more than a catastrophe
And you never really deserved a life

Daily challenges

Another day, another dollar
24 hours but I didn't grow taller
Things look a little bit rough
Tidy up? Let's leave it, close enough

Dancehall hero

I'm learning to do the Tango
Like it's never been done before
It was written a long time ago
By someone who knew the score
You hold the girl ever so close
Then you spin her all around
Lift your head, point your nose
And make yourself feel proud
The next one we dance is the Waltz
It was composed by Herr Strauss
Who was always ever so stolz
His music earned great applause
But the last dance of the night
Is always what is called Rock 'n Roll
It's considered a musical blight
When someone sings – bless my soul
But now the dancing is over
The evening is getting real late
And you think you're in clover
When she agrees to another date
So you wait till the next weekend
While your heart is all aflutter
And you hope when next you dance
Your legs do not turn to butter

Dancing moves

Music plays most every day
It makes me sway and dance
And people watch and call me gay
As it seems so at first glance
But I can tell you here and now
That is really not the case
Just look at this pretty one
Who brightened up on my face.

Darkness ahead

Where have all the flowers gone
Oh Lord, what have we done
The singers all stopped singing
The church bells have stopped ringing
The future once so bright, is gone

Dashing ones hopes

Darling, while I am at the shops
Is there something you want me to get
Yes, sweetie, you have raised my hopes
For recognition and a bit of respect
That would be just so terrific
And give me such cause to cheer
Well, babe, you need to be more specific
Is it some wine or a carton of beer?

Dawn

The stars have lost their distant light,
the sun comes up, so large and bright.
The sky is a pale, clear and blue
the mountains shrouded in a distant hue.
While I sit in the shade of a tree
it's green, as far as the eye can see.
I hear the quiet babble of the brook,
it's as pretty as a child's picture book.
As out into the world I gaze,
it reminds me of my childhood days,
when I shook with wonder and with fear
the first time that I saw a deer.
Or the time I came to the top of a hill
and saw a lake, so clear and still.
Then when sitting there in the shade,
watched the wildlife down in the glade.
And regardless of the kind of weather,
it was always beautiful in the heather.
My mind reaches out way past any fence
and I hope this day just never ends.

Day dreams

Long ago, yet not so far away
I remember it like yesterday
We were foolish and oh so young
Words of love rolled off our tongue
Words we said as if we knew
Just when our dreams would come true
But those years have passed away
And there's little more that I can say
And as there's nothing more that's new
I'll just dream my dreams of you
With memories that are mine to keep
I shall kiss you once more in my sleep

Daylight saving

There was a time, well not quite so fluid
When saints and kings exacted revenge
To tell the seasons it took the Druids
To build what is known as Stonehenge
In those days it would have been a crime
To move time forward or even back
Say what you will, they now change time
But at Stonehenge they stopped keeping track
Beginning of summer there are men with beards
And women bearing golden coloured locks
There is dancing and songs can be heard
They're moving stones to adjust the clock
Come autumn it seems that quite by chance
And perhaps with the help of Merlin's ghost
It gives the mystery a touch of romance
While quite a few of the stones have been lost
Now the feeling of seasons is really mixed up
And time and space just feel so dull
It is the same when you look into a cup
Wondering, is it half empty or really half full

Death row

Don't ever ask to walk in my shoes
I was a killer who is paying his dues
Sentenced to death, no mercy or parole
That's what you get when you have no soul
Don't cry for me, my life it is done
Me and Hell now will be as one
I understand why the Devil does grin
For it's time now to pay for my sins

Destiny!

He was the Senator for Illinois
Not someone who rode on the range
He had a vision as a man not as a boy
And he called it – Time for a change
Now he stands before his nation
American through and through
Here to fulfill his destination
President of the Red, White and Blue
America has made their choice
And now as President forty-four
Soon we will hear his strong voice
As he opens histories door!

Destiny

When I die with the Lord I have a date
Will He smile or will He wear a frown
Will it matter if I am gay or I'm straight
Will I get thorns or will I wear a crown
I believe we are all children of His
A semblance of what He has made
Yet humans think it is hit or miss
But I would rather think it is fate

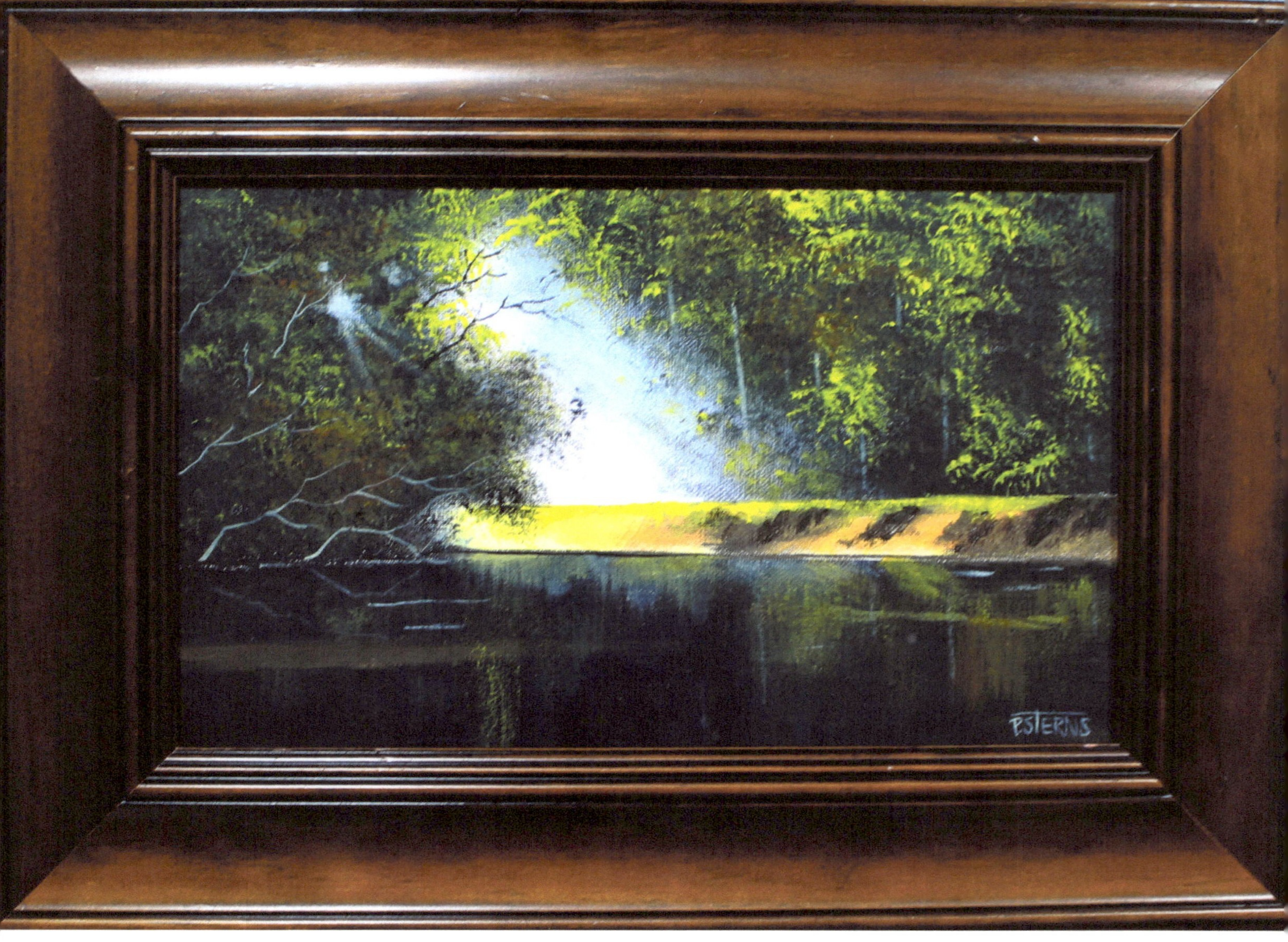
P.STERNS

Difference of opinion!

A friend of mine and I were discussing sex just the other day
And he explained that at sixty two for a miracle he'd have to pray!
I said that sixty odd wasn't all that old and better still,
You are only as old as the woman that you feel.
I know, I know, he said with a voice laden with dismay
I can't get junior to perform, even if I were to pay!
You guessed it, he said, I even gave the Viagra stuff a try
But the truth is that junior and me, simply don't see eye to eye!

Different times

In years gone by as I recall
They used to sing and dance
A gay time had by one and all
With life, work and romance
A gay time now, and so I've heard
And I tell you ridgy didge
Turns out simply to be a word
For an ice cream in your fridge

Disappointments in life

Everyone wants to go to Heaven
But nobody wants to die
I heard this when I was seven
But at 10 I learned to cry
There was no Father Christmas
No Easter Bunny to be found
And I took a wild guess
No-one returns once they're in the ground
Everyone wants to go to Heaven
But nobody wants to die
And now at ninety-seven
I've learned that pigs don't fly

About John Laws

Dr. Democracy

The man with the golden tonsils
the man upon the throne,
he is there in his mighty fortress,
behind the golden microphone.

He is known throughout the country,
his opinions are either hated or revered.
The Emu sings about him
and all over the country he is heard.

He doesn't care about politics,
his own conclusions he draws,
the man who has irreverent logic,
there is no one like John Laws.

Inspired by a TV show where
A person donated their heart before dying.

The donor

Praise the Lord in the Heavens above
as he is merciful and full of love,
for someone is getting a brand new start,
because another died and gave his heart.

Dreams

You once held my heart in your hand
As I laid my love at your feet
And the day your life came to an end
You left me so the Lord you could meet
But now as we are unable to speak
All that I have left is my dreams
At times I find the comfort I seek
Out there among those lovely moon beams
And while I am there in open space
There is the answer to what I hope to find
I'm greeted by a smile that's on your face
And the touch of love that you left behind
But come the morrow, it is a new day
And reality is slowly sinking in
All I can do now is hope and pray
The lottery of life will grant me a win

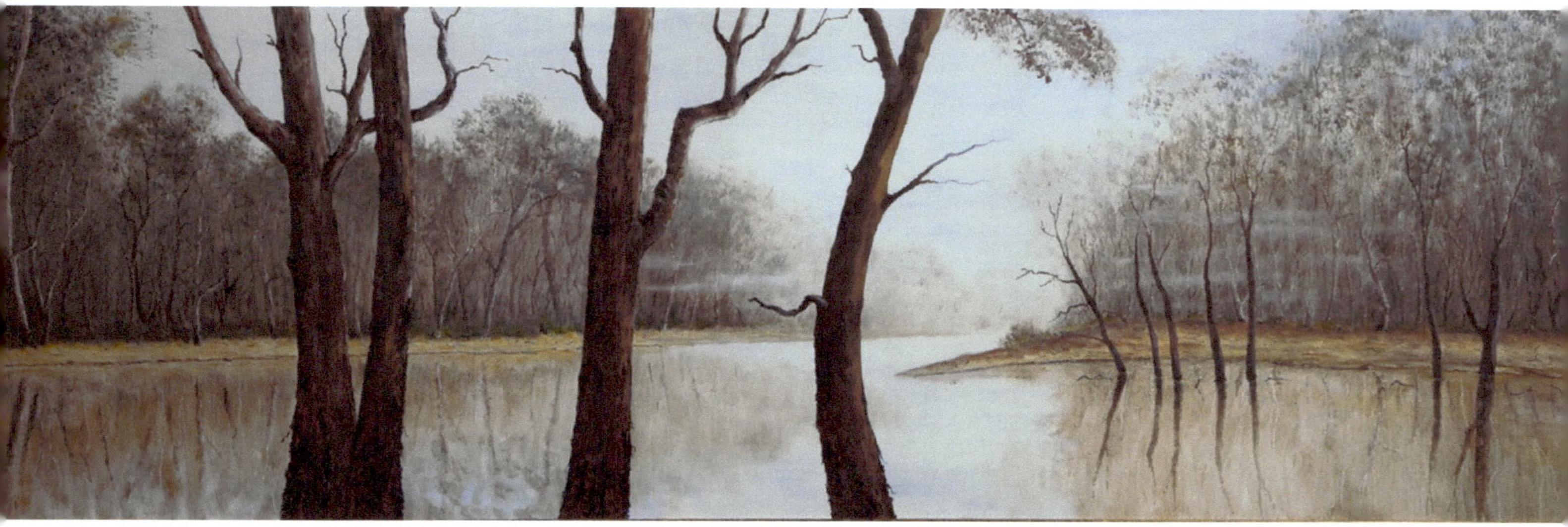

Dreaming

Where do they go, the dreams that come
Deep in the dark of night
Where often I am bound to roam
And sometimes I even fight
What is it that can make a man
Do evil in that state
And come the morning, when
He can't remember what awaits
Other times, as if by design
The greatest human he's become
Who can wine and dine
And is praised for what he's done
Yet none of that means anything
They are remnants in our mind
That often like the truth will ring
And somehow got left behind

Dreams

When I was just a baby in my mother's arms
I got by with smiles and my boyish charms.
I went to school, learned to read and write
Loved to run, but hated to fight.
One day I hoped on my path I'd go far
But that's the way dreams are.
So when I got married, I had always hope
That no matter what, I would be able to cope.
But now that I have children and a wife
I sometimes feel a disappointment with life.
I had dreams of riches, nice cars, and a big home
Now it would seem, that dream is gone.
But wait a minute, this is not how it ends
I have a family, grandsons and some nice friends.
I have hobbies and I even learned to paint,
Heaven forbid that I turn out to be a saint.
One could hope I might be a rising star,
But than again, that's how dreams are.

Dreams of tomorrow

I'd love to hear the angels singing
I'd love to see them kneel and pray
I'd love to see that chariot swinging
Way down low on my final day
And I know you're bound to hear it
As I lay me down on the ground to die
Fought for freedom, what became of it
Here on those lonely fields of Athenry
I used to dream of a great tomorrow
But all that's left now is tears and pain
My love only feels the sorrow
For now we will never love again
Can you tell me why I had to die
And why she is now all alone
Tell my why she sat there and cried
While I lie here beneath this stone.

Dreams

No matter how far I have travelled
I have looked but couldn't find
The mystery would not unravel
Of pictures I see in my mind.

Places so peaceful and others so wild
My daddy spoke of he'd seen
Pictures he painted in a child's mind
Stories that were like a dream

When I grew up I travelled the world
I searched but I couldn't find
Than I managed to find a girl
Who was graceful, loving and kind.

And now I find as I grow old
The journey's not over it seems
Because the stories I've told
Are pictures in my children's dreams

Drifting along

Oh my dreams will always wander
And at times I feel that I'm alone
At times I'm out in the blue yonder
But more often in the land where I was born.
But my kids don't share these feelings
They don't know that they're alive
Hardly managing day to day dealings
Without purpose, a husband or a wife.
My wife and I find more each day to share
And it almost seems to be a shame
That only about each other we now care
But life has become a survivor game.
Even if with relations and life we disagree
There are friends and we still have some,
They say the best things in life are free,
But we have each other and the green grass of home.
No use wondering what the future brings
But how to stay warm when it is cold,
It doesn't matter who dances or who sings,
It's all part of life and getting old.

Drinking and driving

Don't be like a bull at the gate
It doesn't matter if you are late
It's important to stay alive
So if you are drinking, don't drive
You might be lucky with just a fine
But if not – could be dead on time.

Dr Pepper

**Dr Pepper, Dr Pepper, how fond I am of you,
I have tried the others, there were only two.
Coca Cola and Pepsi, you might have guessed,
But why drink them and miss out on the best.**

Drugs

Sex, drugs and Rock 'n Roll
Have always taken their toll
I can't believe what someone said
If you're not LIVING, you're better off dead
But what LIVING is, if you will
Is taking a mysterious little pill
Or sticking a needle in your arm
Knowing it WILL do you harm
And that for certain makes you a mug
I prefer LIFE as my choice of drug

End of days

A picture's worth a thousand words
It's what they say, it's what I heard
But a lonely guy can't paint a single thing
They say loneliness loves company
But one is one not two or three
If only this darn phone would ring
There were kisses, hugs and afterglow
But that was then and this is now
Where have all the good times really gone
Now we're getting older each and every day
And despite what all the people day
We're staring at the slowly setting sun

End of the line

Tell me the things that matter
And what you want me to be
And I'll write you a letter
Of the world that I can see
I've burned all your old love letters
That you once wrote to me
For you want to be a go-getter
All alone and fancy free
I know one day you'll find
When you're looking down the track
It is my love you left behind
And crying won't get it back

Endless

The sands of time are passing through
The road to who knows where
Yet there we stood and said I do
It was long ago and far away
The thoughts that keep crossing our mind
Are they blessings or are they a curse
No matter which no solace do they bring
Nor do they quench our thirst
The universe and all its many stars
Cares not for the heart or feels the pain
How could it if it counts all those wars
And sees the foolishness of men
Just look at Valhalla, look at Heaven
It's filled with warriors standing toe to toe
Every one of them laughing and bragging
Still daring each other for another go
Be it a rifle now or an old spear
A modern man or one from a cave
No cry for peace do I ever hear
And there's none found in a grave

Equality of life

Come all yee faithful and you overachievers
Even all you nutters and you non-believers
Two thousand years have slowly passed in time
Some trust in God while others think it is a crime
How many more years will be spent at war
How much more suffering is there left to endure
Each passing year we believe and live in hope
Some in abundance while others barely cope
How many millions do you need to survive
While others are begging just to stay alive
There is tennis, golf, soccer and a game called cricket
The money that they earn is simply more than wicked
Lotteries that promise you a certain change of life
While others find everything has taken a big dive
I have no idea what 2019 for us has in store
But I'm sure the rich, will simply pray for more.

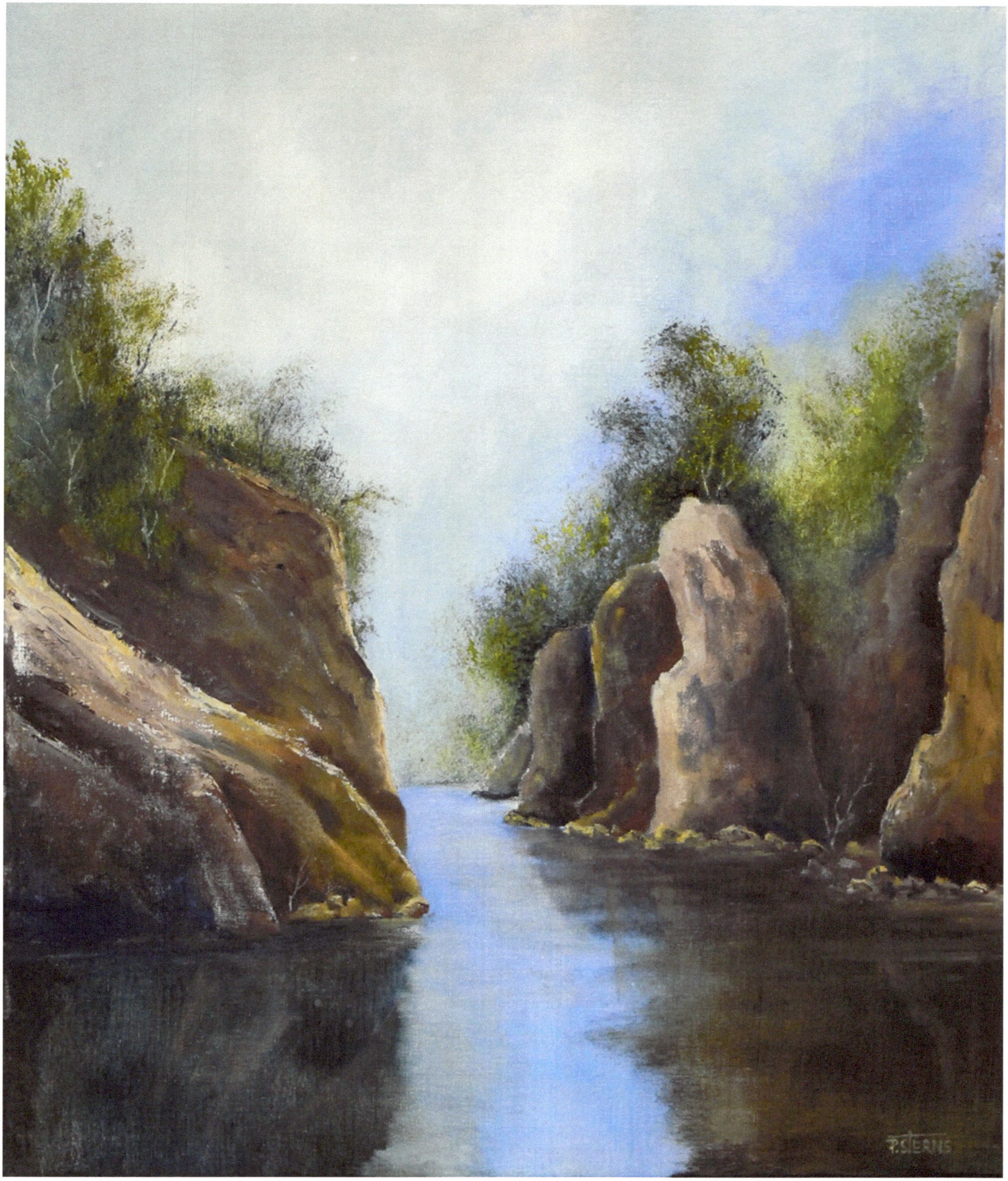
P. STERNS

Evolution

Today I joined the human race
That is, as far as I can tell
One of them with a hairy face
The other one did really smell
Some have said that we are cousins
That isn't something to shout about
The first one had something called bosoms
While the other one had a snout
One says that he has your back
And the other one agrees
One of them will smoke some crack
While the first one shoots the breeze
Oh maker of all this creation
What am I to do with this
When all this here misinformation
Is somewhat short of bliss
I'd rather stay what I am
Well, whatever that might be
Then be something called a man
Or just some monkey in a tree.

Fairy land

How do we know where we're going
How do we know what is real
When do the cold winds start blowing
And how does loneliness feel
Someone always has answers
They know just how you must feel
They say you will feel better
Because if you don't, nobody will
So I now believe in the moment
Where fairies fly through the sky
Believe me it is quite common
But don't bother asking me why.

Fairy tales

Oh dear me, what were the stories I was told
Of dragons, wizards and knights so brave and bold
But could it be that they once were real
For its clashing swords I hear and magic I can feel
I have dreamt of them, up there in Camelot
Of that magic place, that time has now forgot
When they spoke of Arthur, their king and lord
The only one who wielded Excalibur, his sword
It was a time when Merlin walked upon the land
And knights who fought with swords in their hand
But somehow this all vanished, like a dried up stream
Only to be remembered by children in their dreams

The fare

**In the days of the Romans and Greeks
you had the Ferryman of the Styx,
to take your soul across the divide
to that great unknown at the other side.
For when one died, one could not tell,
if it was to Heaven or to Hell.
One was either saved, or one would burn
after being ferried across that river of no return.
There were souls, who couldn't pay the fare,
others still, who just did not care.
For when they lived, you could hear them tell,
that they didn't believe in Heaven or in Hell.
But since the birth of Jesus Christ,
the belief in the Ferryman has somewhat died.
But if you believe, tell me if you can,
who actually pays the Ferryman?**

The farmer

Oh what a frightening noisy wonder,
first a flash, then the might thunder.
You replay the lightning in your mind's eye
as the thunder rolls through the clouds in the sky.
At first as a drizzle, then in mighty drops
the rain gives life to the thirsty fields and crops.
It would seem the earth stands still,
as Thor displays his might will.
When the noise of thunder rumbles in the clouds,
you don't see any admiring crowds.
Even the strongest man can tremble with fear
when the lightning's crack he first can hear.
But then the noise and rain will start to fade,
the farmer says a silent prayer and he is glad,
that the heavens opened up and gave him rain,
saving him from worry, anguish and pain.
And as he looks around he gives a might sigh
for there before him is a great rainbow in the sky.
He feels warmth embrace his heavy heart,
thankful to the Lord for a brand new start.

Father time

What makes us worry and creases our brow?
What turns a young person into an old one now?
Is it old father time, or is it old age?
With all this wisdom, why am I not a sage?
The fact that you lived, had children, a wife,
Doesn't make any difference at the end of your life.
You might have power and
possessions, money and gold,
But no matter what, they can't
stop you from getting old!
Some think they can actually win the race
If some young women they can chase.
They have a facelift and dye their hair,
And then complain that life isn't fair.
That now, when they finally reached the top,
It comes to an end and has to stop.
Whether in Culcutta, where life doesn't get cheaper,
Or on a throne, we all have to
face the Grim Reaper!
You can live in Hawaii or behind the Iron Curtain,
But from the day you're born,
only one thing is certain,
That one day you will sip from that bitter cup
And realise, when your time is up – it's up!
So wipe away the frown that creases your face,
You know you are old, so show some grace!
Be an example to the younger generation,
Tell them to live their life with a passion.
Because with each passing day,
they don't get younger.
So live truthfully, with respect and honour.
And every so often, on your own accord,
Go to church and give thanks to the Lord.
Now enjoy the autumn in your life that you have,
Don't waste your time and rant and rave.
Make peace with the Lord, family and friends,
So that your life meant something when it ends!

Feeling blue!

I have a family and a wife at home
So why do I sit here and feel so alone?
It so happens that just the other day
I heard a little girl's voice say:
"How far is heaven and can I visit my dad?"
Those few words left me ever so sad.
I've often had those thoughts myself
When the midnight clock strikes twelve!
And are there windows in heaven to look down?
And if dad saw me, would he frown?
Or would a smile grace his face
When he sees me in this place?
Would he approve of what I've become?
Would he be proud to call me his son?
What the answer could be, I cannot say
So I'll have to wait until it's my day
When I go to that place up in the sky
And to my family I say goodbye.
So until the day I'm called by God
I shall be happy with what I've got!
But it's my birthday that is true
And I don't have a reason to be blue!
I have grandkids, children, friends and a wife,
So why be blue – happiness is being alive!

Feeling good!

You may be true and faithful
Live life without a care
But you need to be careful
For the devil wants his share
It has been said time and again
And this is nothing new
To help relieve the taste of pain
The devil will visit you
Cast ye not your evil eye
On those who pray for peace
Lest you wish to pay the price
On that final judgment day
Don't let the bird of paradise
Fly up your nose real soon
Or you will know it wasn't wise
To dance to a different tune

Fighting the blues

The gulf of life is getting wider every day
No matter how hard you try, you can't win
It seems you're always facing the wrong way
It's hard to believe and harder still to grin
They say that life's like a bowl of cherries
So nice, so rich and ever so sweet
But you find nothing but trouble and worries
And it's impossible to stand on your own feet
Your friends say that you suffer from the blues
You need to change and simply cheer up
You pray someone would give them the news
And tell them I wish that they would shut up
For depression can hit you any old time
And if you're thinking your own life to end
There's no reason to believe it's the end of the line
Call someone or better still, talk to a friend
Talk to someone and tell them how you feel
For we all get the blues now and then
There's no one here that's the man of steel
What you need is understanding and a helping hand

Finding love

Never go looking for a lover
That has left you in the night
Love should be for the asking
If you say the words just right
For with too much expectation
A romance gets out of hand
What could be life's sensation
Is just a one night stand
For you can't make someone love
Just because you feel you do
A one sided love is not enough
It's like running with just one shoe
But if your senses are reeling
And your heart is beating like a drum
And if she shares your feelings
She'll be there when the daylight come.

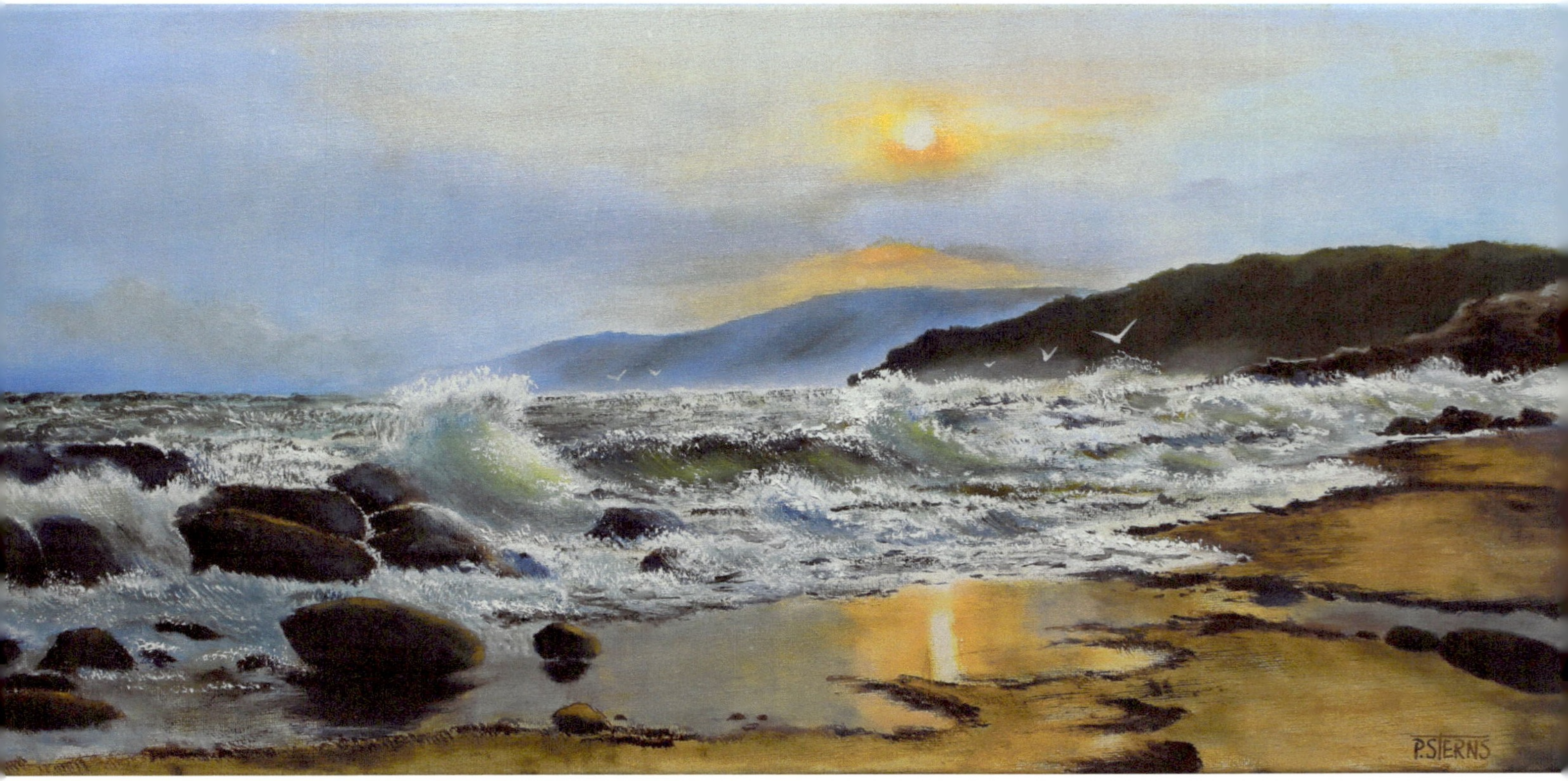
P.STERNS

Finding the way back

My mind found peace in the sunshine
Of the warm California sun
After the girl that I thought was mine
Had left me in Texas alone
My heart used to soar like an eagle
Up there in the clear blue sky
And I thought that just like that eagle
My love could learn how to fly
But now I feel like a sparrow
That cannot fly or make a sound
My heart is pierced by an arrow
And is lying there dead on the ground
At first I cried me an ocean
And I prayed to the heavens above
Then someone gave me a potion
That cured me of the heartache and love
Now her memory is just a memory
And I no longer think it's a curse
My mind is clear and it's free
And at peace with the whole universe!

California is on fire, how sad the world

Fire in the canyon!

A single spark on the ground
Where care should have been employed
Here once beauty was found
All now by the fire destroyed!
It lights up the sky by night
The trees they are dying in pain
Oh what a terrible sight
Mother Nature is praying for rain!

Follow the call

I heard that two friends of mine
Have gone on the eternal way
They went the way of old Father Time
Who counts our every day.
But I believe the day will come
When I meet family, friends and all
It will be when my work is done
And I heed Father Time's last call!

Food

I'm a man who really likes his food
And there's something I'd like to say
I found Mexican tastes really good
I can eat it each and every day
Now despite the worlds troubles and strife
I make salsa with tomatoes, peppers and lime
And intend to spend the rest of my life
Sitting and eating one taco at a time

Footsteps of the past

Who's footsteps are we following,
are they big or are they small?
Is there someone calling,
is there anyone at all?

We often think and wonder
as most of us do, I trust:
What's out there in that blue yonder
that we can't see, but trust?

To me my mother once had said :
Like a child in God you have to trust,
so keep it in your mind, your head,
Remember, He comes first.

So you do your best, you sing and pray
but often you just forget,
that from God, in some small way,
an answer you WILL get.

The footsteps we have followed throughout time,
are not your fathers, nor mine,
but we find that when we step aboard,
they are the footsteps of Jesus, our Lord.

Footsteps of the past

Who's footsteps are we following,
are the big or are the small?
Is there someone calling,
is there anyone at all?
We often think and wonder
as most of us do, I trust:
What's out there in that blue yonder
that we can't see, but trust.
Is there a kind of heaven,
is there a kind of hell ?
It is clear that by living,
we certainly can't tell.
To me my mother once had said :
Like a child in God you have to trust,
so keep it in your mind, your head,
Remember, He comes first.
So you do your best, you sing and pray
but often you forget,
that from God, in some small way,
an answer you WILL get.
So once our life has gone,
in the Bible we are told,
God will send His only Son,
to take us in His fold.
So the footsteps we followed throughout time,
are not your fathers, nor mine,
but we find that when we step aboard,
they are the footsteps of Jesus, our Lord.

For all lovers

Another year has come and gone
but our love, it goes on and on,
for now and for all time,
you will be my Valentine.

For the defence

Hello old buddy, old pal
The one defending George Pell
Who called it nothing but lies
Expressed against two young boys
And speaking in the past tense
Called it just a vanilla offence
I wonder if that really were true
What will you call it if performed on you

Forever lonesome

He's standing there all alone
And has done so for some years
He wishes that he had a son
Or that he could shed some tears
His coat is old and torn
His shoes they hide the holes
In the socks that he has worn
Since they took away his soul
So he stands there, rain or shine
With his lips forever sealed
There's a great sadness in his mind
For he's just a scarecrow in the field

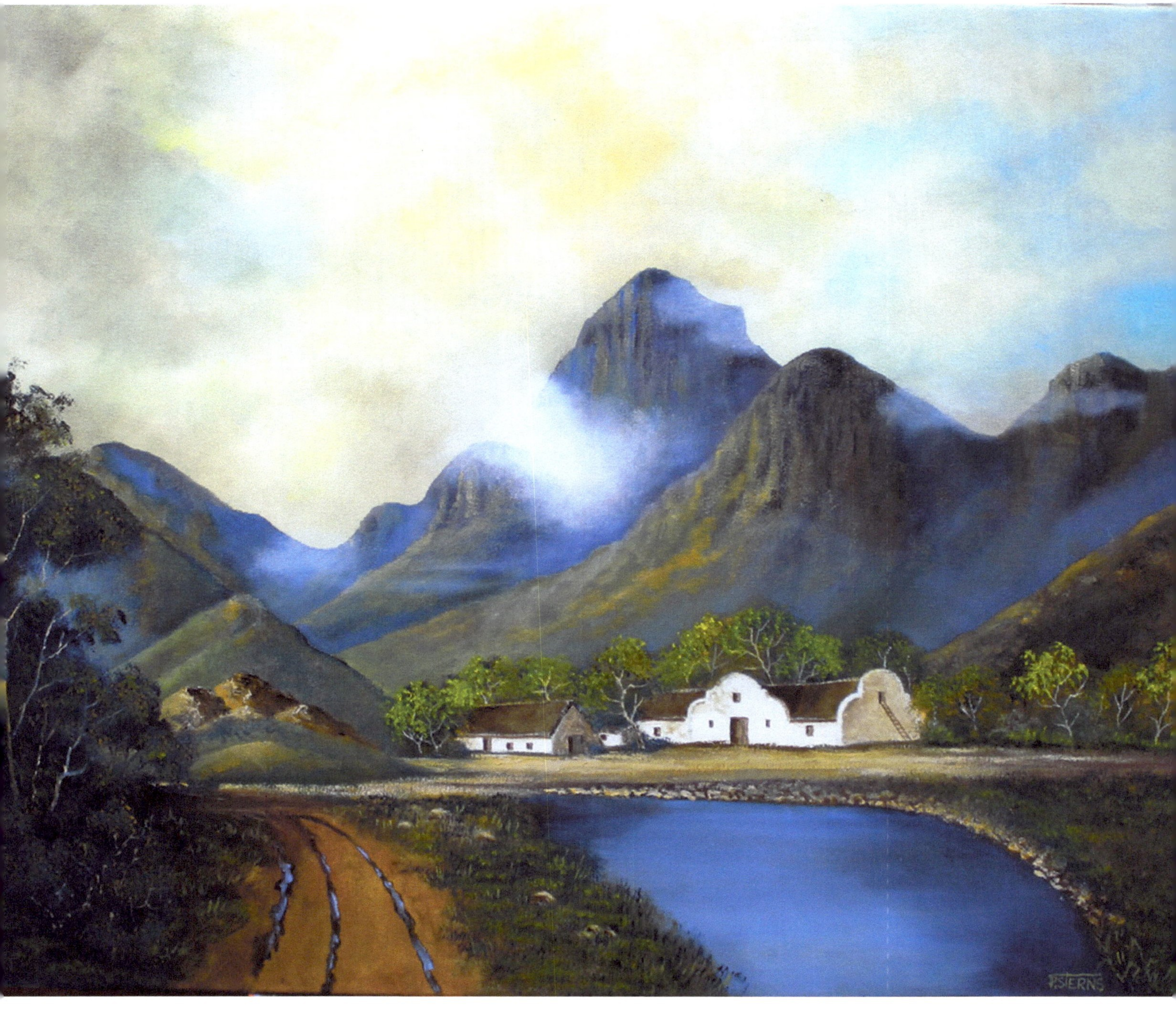

Forever love

If I told you that I loved you
Would you tell me that you're mine
Would you say you love me too
And make the sun forever shine
The question asked, the pondering kind
It seems to just roll off the tongue
It plagues the uncertain mind
When you are foolish and young
But now the years have passed
And my hair is sparse and grey
You know that her love did last
And nothing will take that away

Freeloader

There once was a man by the name of Bud
Who liked beer that frothed, looked like suds.
He even thought of the bar as a geyser,
So when he didn't pay, the miser,
after a beating, I wonder, was Bud wiser?

Friday 13th

There are movies, books and stories
about Friday the 13th and the worries
that are caused by just this date,
especially if you see a black cat.

It would seem you are out of luck
if you park you car under a truck,
but otherwise, all I can say,
this is just another day.

And bad luck or not,
the whole thing is just rot
and after all's been said and done
it's a Friday and a three behind a one.

Friendship and love!

There comes a time that we must one day all pass away
And it matters little just how much we kneel and pray
There is a question in my mind as to who is next and why
When I talk to my friends do I simply smile or cry
But I do believe that friendship will last for all of time
It's just like love that is meant for your heart and mine
But when the hand of time hits that final note
All that we can say is – that is all she wrote!
For each day of our life is a new leaf in a book
And once a page is read there is no turning back
The only lesson we need learn is to cherish friends and love
For there is little else we can take with us to our grave!

DA, our friend in the USA

Friendship

To hear the voice of a friend
Over distance and time,
Is like breaking lent
By eating bread and drinking wine.
Friendship that reaches across the ocean
Is something that cannot be bought
Stirs the heart with deep emotion,
Is the one thing that cannot be taught.
It is something you feel, again and again,
When one look, one clasp of the hand
Overcomes hardship and pain,
But remains friendship till the end.
It's like the promise of the Lord
Who lives in the Heavens above,
That friendship is not just a word,
But unconditional love.

The future

It's Remembrance Day once again
When we recall fallen friends and foe.
For some they can still feel the pain
Although it's so many years ago.
America is getting good and ready
To fight Iraq on your behalf
The churches are collecting for the needy
No one sees that of fighting we had enough.
On this day we pretend to grieve for the dead
And stand there, heads bowed in sorrow.
But why not use our energies instead
For a life together, today and tomorrow?

Future and past

I can't forget the past
How I wish that I could
And I thought it would last
For you said our love was good
You can't see the future
And you can't change the past
I still can't forget your
How I wish it would last
The years they have gone
But the memories remain
They're just like a song
With an haunting refrain
Now the angels have spoken
Reminding me of my past
Memories were awoken
Of a love that didn't last
But you can't see ahead
The past is the past once again
And when you are dead
The future and the past are the same.

Future trends

With the help of a little bit of DNA
We'll be able to put our knives away.
Our teeth we can as useless render
The steaks we eat will be ever so tender.

The tiger and the lion they won't need their claws,
Soon they can eat their meat using paper straws.
And if we continue and get it really good,
We'll be able to just inhale all of our future food.

This is regression and not evolution
But Mr Howard has found the only solution
We can live in a bottle or in a plastic cube
While he feeds us bullshit through a little tube.

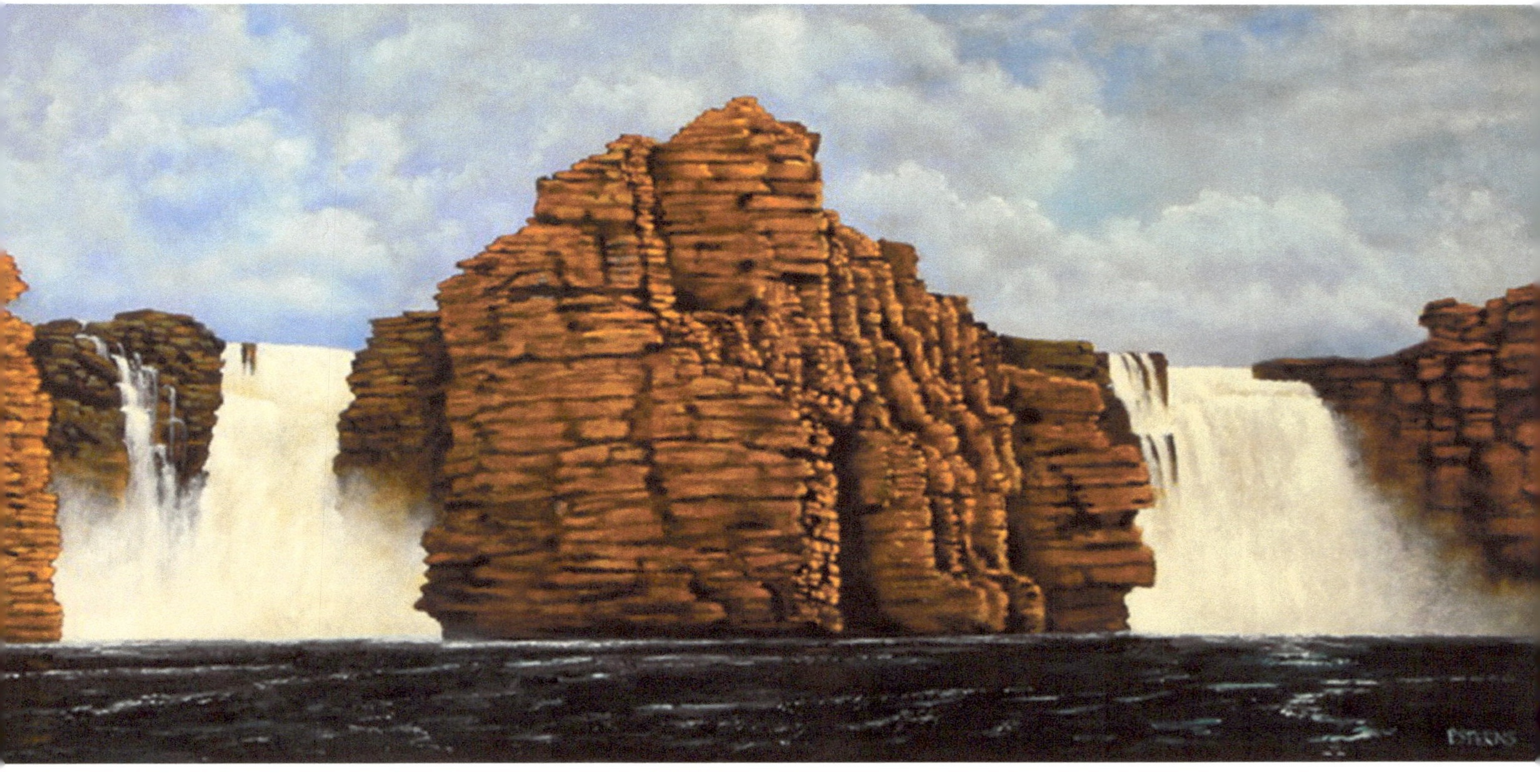

Get even

If you've been jilted or just left alone,
and your loving heart has turned to stone,
there's one way this chapter one closes,
with black paper, wrapped around 13 dead roses.

Getting old

Once there was a time when
A child's spirit would soar
Up with the clouds, the rain
There where the thunder would roar
Oh how the times have changed
Where once there were dreams
It is chaos, all is rearranged
No fulfilment at all it seems
But now the child is a man
The future takes on a new goal
It all happened one day when
He discovered to have a soul
He learned to have new dreams
To cope with love and with tears
But despite it all, it seems
He grew old throughout the years
Now the future is as dim as his eyes
And the child's dreams faded away
But now he thinks he is wise
Knowing dreams end with the break of day
Once there was so much to live for
Once there were family and friends
But that once isn't there anymore
And one day all dreaming just ends

Getting old!

Farewell my darling I'm off to that distant shore
It has been a dream of mine, since I was a kid of four!
The grass is greener on the other side, so I have been told
And I want to get me some of that before I am too old!
They say the women over there are as sweet as apple pie
It never rains, that the sun just shines from a clear blue sky.
Nobody ever has to work because the streets are paved with gold
And I want to get me some of that before I am too old!
When I got there friends, I found the women looked just fine
But they were all too busy doing nothing to pass the time.
Even my best pitches, charm and flowers left everyone cold
I wanted me some of that, but they say that I'm just too old!
I was going to write you darling, but I couldn't find a store
To buy paper and some lead before my pencil won't write no more
But I'm coming home instead before all my dreams grow cold
And you say I can't cut the mustard because I truly am too old!

Glory day!

As I dream of a new tomorrow
Angels sing my last request
No more tears, pain or sorrow
Now that they lay me down to rest
Oh how sweet the voices calling
All my family at the gate
Just how far I could have fallen
Had I left it up to fate
Jesus said that He would save me
Now I'm standing at the throne
And I'm basking in the glory
Of the Father and the Son!

Go on

I've done everything that I can
To get her off my mind
But every now and than
There's a memory I find
I look at a distant star
Just like lovers often do
A golden ring has turned to dust
And brown eyes now are blue
Go on, just keep goin' on
Time never does stand still
Look for the rising sun
Coming over that distant hill
I can drink a little beer
Watch the TV and the news
But that doesn't bring me cheer
Or ever wash away the blues
So go on and keep going on
Even cry a little if you must
Every night has a new dawn
And lets mem'ries turn to dust!

Going for PM

Years ago so it would seem
Someone said – I – had – a – dream
But this is now, not then
And we have someone who – has a plan

Going home!

The pain of a young man's foolish heart
It can cloud a sunny day
How many years have we been apart
They are more than I can say!
And when the day finally comes
For me to really see
I'll go home to the ones
That sit and wait for me!
My mother she's been crying
A sea of bitter tears
And my father has been dying
For many lonesome years
But now the son's going home
For there seems no other choice
And all the pain will be gone
We will sing with just one voice
We'll give thanks to the Lord above
And see what must be seen
We'll rejoice in our new found love
And forget what might have been!

Greatest story

I cannot see what lies there yonder
I cannot hear what wasn't said
But sometimes I just sit and wonder
Where will I be once I am dead
Will there be flowers up in Heaven
Will my relations take me hold
Will there be more blessings I'll be given
That'll be the greatest story ever told!

Hanging on

Life has all these ups and downs
Great big smiles, sad old frowns
Kids have grown, they're all gone
I don't need no mem'ries hanging on
Those mem'ries once were nice
Father Time told me – no dice
Pretty soon you too will be gone
And won't need no mem'ries hanging on
But who can tell when that will be
We'll just have to wait and see
So until the day that I'm gone
Life's mem'ries will keep on hanging on

Hans Heysen

The years have slowly faded
The colors once so true
His work so much debated
By people, as they often do
A pasture or perhaps a tree
Will leave the viewers guessin'
If what they are about to see
Are the footsteps of Hans Heysen?

Happy anniversary

Dance with me darling
Before we forget
And all of our memories
Turn to thoughts of regret
All these years together
So let's take a chance
Let's think of forever
And have one more dance!

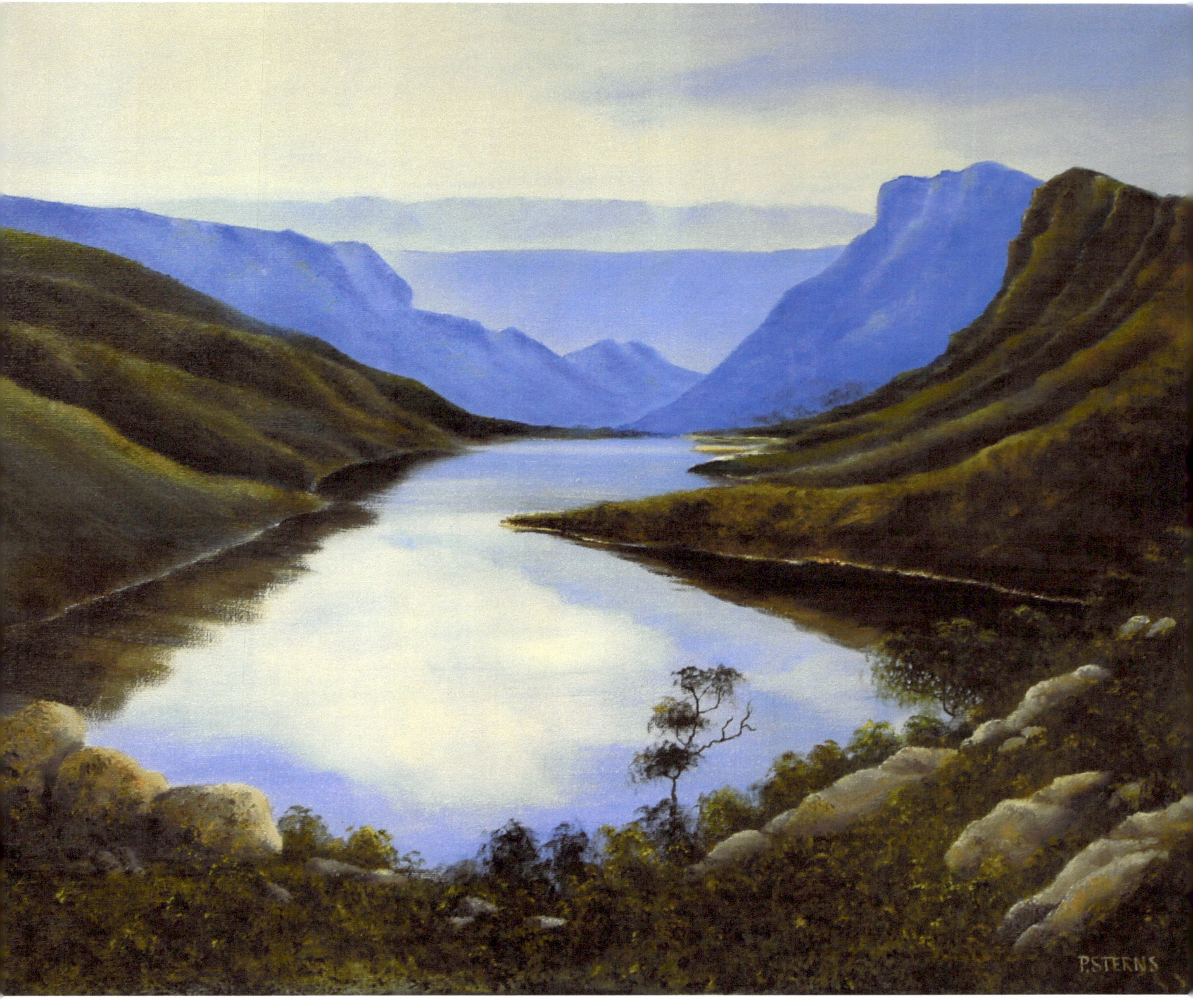
P.STERNS

Having it all

One day forever will be over
And then he'll try to find a way
To change that little four leaf clover
For just one, just one more day
Never happy with what he's been given
Never enough of what he's got
Some people they go on living
Always unhappy with their lot
A villa white on the Riviera
A host of friends in every port
He drives a humble Porsche Carrera
And is an ace in every sport
Yet he often dreams and wonders why
When he goes to sleep at night
And the stars light up the sky
There is no love to hold him tight
He has it all, he has too much
But has no children, has no wife
No tender kisses, no gentle touch
Oh what a lonely, lonely life

Heart of stone

Where are you, oh love of mine
It has been quite a while
Since we promised till the end of time
And you walked down the aisle
Years have come, years have gone
Wrinkles on my aging brow
Hair that's bleached by the sun
Are proof of the here and now
Yet memories still haunt my mind
I've searched every cranny, every nook
No matter what, I cannot find
My heart that you once took
So please help me someone
Help me somehow to be brave
To carry this great lump of stone
Called a heart, down to my grave

Heaven

Tell me not that I am failing
It's Heaven's door that I now see
As my aching soul is ailing
For where I am now meant to be
The door is gleaming in the light
And I can hear the angels sing
What a wonderful and moving sight
As they glide along on silent wings
Now my heartbeat it is racing
And I know I am not alone
For the One that I am facing
Is telling me that I am home

Highway of life

We used to fight a little
When we didn't see eye to eye
Then we would love a little
And now life has passed us by
While I think of those times, my dear
They are precious memories of the past
No more happy laughter I can hear
Sadly life goes on and never lasts
Sometimes words echo in my mind
Like, hello love, how have you been
But they pass just like the wind
That can be felt but never seen
Fleeting moments that are so rare
Of a kind and gentle woman's love
You can hope but you can never dare
That eternity could ever be enough
May the memories of those bygone years
Sustain you through the passing days
So as your destination nears
You know it's the end of life's highway

Hindsight

If only I'd called the nurse
Things might not have got worse
No need to cry and curse
While lying here in a hearse
Too late now, life to rehearse

His own!

I hear this heavenly voice
I see footprints here in the sand
I know I have this choice
To leave or take hold of His hand.
Here in the Garden of Eden
I sit under the old olive tree
And I feel peace and freedom
And I think He is talking to me.
In the distance church bells are ringing
My heart it feels filled with joy
I think I can hear angels singing
I'm like a child with a new toy.
You can say what you will about Jesus
Was he really the son of the Lord?
Not since the time of Moses
Has someone listened to His word!
But you can't help but wonder
When you feel the touch of His hand
You hear the roar of distant thunder
Or see footprints right here in the sand.
I walk to the mountains up yonder
Past this dusty, ancient old town
I look up to the Heavens and wonder
One day will He call me his own?

Homeland

Where the hills of my childhood
Look down on the dale
Where the mist of the morning
Is as gentle as a veil
Where my mother first held me
And where the tall pines grow
Is where you will find me
In the midsummer suns glow
I shall always remember it
And I will till the day I die
The country of my birth
Is worth every tear in my eye
There are those that remember
And there are those who forget
But when your life reaches September
You will recall it with regret!

Hope

A caravan travels through the night
Trying to find the newborn king
The only guide a star in the sky
To find hope the newborn shall bring
Times are so much different now
And yet they are still the same
I'd like to think that we somehow
Have learned the infant's name
An outback man with a horse and cart
Riding to save his stricken wife
If she can get her a brand new heart
There is hope for a better life
Another man, who prays out loud
He's hoping to change mankind's fate
And it pleases him to see the crowd
With no hope but pure blind hate
And here a man who has made a deal
With the law to escape the rope
And this I think, I know, I feel
Is the new caravan of hope?

How come?

Crime doesn't pay like it used to
You can no longer take your fill
The cops are forever looking for you
And jail is now another bitter pill
A cop used to be your friend and neighbour
Across this great and carefree land
All it took for this kind of labour
Was to put some cash in his hand
But now you can't even trust a copper
Just because he wears a star
He is just like any other shopper
With a camera in his brand new car
Now a balaclava and a gun
Can't protect you from a shooting spree
For a copper sitting there in the sun
Is watching you on his colour TV
Yes crime doesn't pay like it used to
But if you listen I will surely tell
I don't know what this world is coming to
For I'm now sitting in this prison cell.

In hope

Now that the Fates of Time have spoken
In voices pure and ever so clear
The Gods of old once more have awoken
And the world again trembles in fear
The warriors through the millennia were brave
And kings are searching for the Golden Fleece
Find the Devil dancing on their grave
A dove in the sky, the fleeting hope of peace
The tears of mothers still fill the seas
Words of prayers drifting upon the air
In the sky with a dove, the bird of peace
Yet the hope of peace, a burden hard to bare

In spirit

If I was the wind, I'd fly so high
As high as the clouds up above
I'd fly through the valley and I'd sigh
But never tell them of my love
And would whisper through the trees
Caress the highest mountain top
And roar across the seven seas
But nothing could make me stop
If I was the wind, I'd kiss your cheek
And you wouldn't know it was me
I'd do it every day of the week
And I would be wild and so free
But I am but a mortal man
I can't fly to those clouds up above
So I'll think of you now and then
And sometimes dream of your love

In the future

There are times you can hear me roar
And there are times when I just sing
Yet the day I reach that distant shore
It will be on those angel's wings
Ask me not what day that be
Come the day, then I will know
Once again my love I'll see
And live forever in the glow
That shines there at the Pearly Gate
At that far and distant shore
Away from all the pain and hate
Awaits God's love forever more

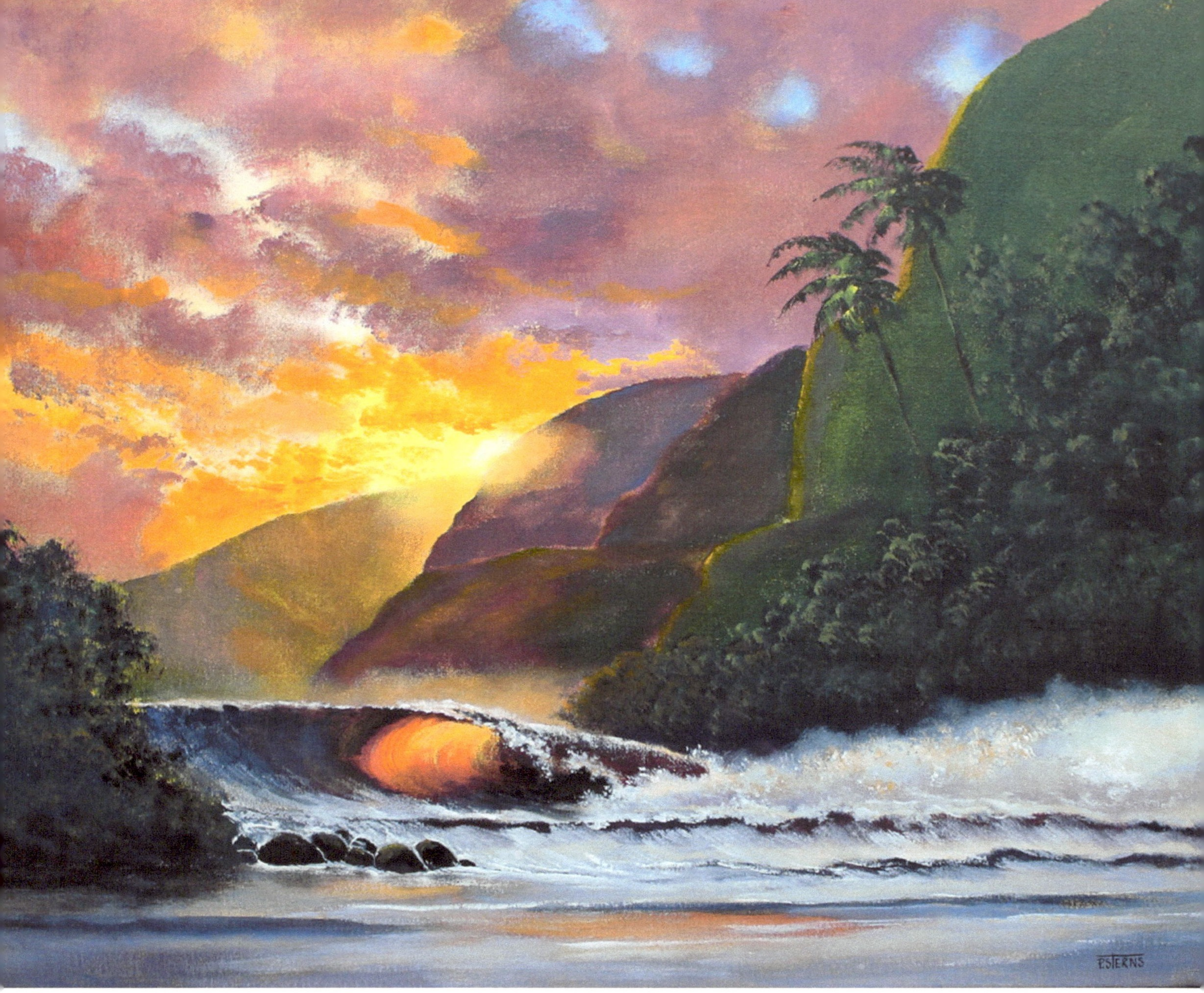
P.STERNS

Is it love?

Should we go our way?
Or should we be right here
Should we leave or stay
And do we really care
How does the wise man know?
What is right or wrong?
Is there an afterglow
When you've a heard a song
When the sun comes up
Does it know when to leave?
When you pick a buttercup
Does the butterfly greave
There's a bird up high
It's almost in the cloud
How does it know how to fly?
Do we know what love is about?
They say love is blind
Yet it starts with a glance
And I guess you'll find
You need to take a chance
So should we go our way?
Or do we stay right here
For if its love we'll stay
And we learn to care.

Jessica

I can spell Caaat!
You can? Yes, C A T, cat.
Do you think I am a fool?
This was my second day in school!

Johnny Cash

How I wish I could have met you
Back when you were so much fun
But I know that it is true
I've heard most all you've ever sung
One day I thought I was in heaven
When I saw this news reel flash
Which was back in nineteen fifty-seven
Someone said – Hi, I'm Johnny Cash
Many years later here Down Under
I saw you singing on the stage
I just watched in awe and wonder
For me you'll always be the rage
Then one day the Highway men
Made a record, made some noise
On the radio I heard you now and then
Singing with Waylon and the boys
But you and Waylon passed away
How I wish we had you back
Why, someone said to me the other day
Did you ever see the Man in Black?
I said – if I ever have a choice
And there is none as far as I can tell
I'd sing along to his voice
Whether I was in Heaven or in Hell.

Just add time

How can you ask where I'm going
If I can't see the road up ahead
Life to me seems to be slowing
At times it feels it's backwards instead
Last time I asked someone – what's up
They said that I was getting old
That I really was no buttercup
And streets were no long paved with gold
Get used to it, for such is life
At times it's hot, now it's cold
They cut the string with a knife
And now my friend, you're old

Kaw-Liga

Someone said I was good for nothin'
Never uttering a single sound
Well I guess I must be good for somethin'
If I am found to stand my ground
I'm gonna catch that midnight rider
I am told it's Paul Revere
He is sipping ice cold cider
While I smell of lukewarm beer
It would be of comfort to me
If he could hear my beckoning call
Perhaps he would see right through me
If I was glass and ten feet tall
But I am just a lonesome cowboy
And my spirit is not free
I am standing on the by-way
I've been carved from on an old pine tree!

I keep on singing

The snow is falling from the sky
And it stirs my imagination,
Why did you have to leave, to die?
What I feel, too much to mention.
The quiet of all that is around
Makes me forget all worldly strife
My heartbeat the only sound
You were my love, my life!
If I could, I'd hold you close
Give thanks for all you gave,
Instead I place a single rose
Upon your snow white grave!
A distant lonely church bell rings
It's Christmas time again.
And now my lonely heart it sings
One day I'll see you once again!
Until that day, I walk alone
The road is there before me.
Until my work on earth is done,
I care for you, as you did for me!
As years will pass, I treasure most
The sound of church bells ringing,
Our love will last, it is not lost,
And my heart will keep on singing!

Keeping memories

The window panes of glass
Let through the morning light
I see glimpses of the past
Shining warm and bright
And like the lark up in the sky
It warms my aching heart
I wish that I could fly
And make a brand new start
But that is something that I seek
And I'll nevermore attain
To reach the highest mountain peek
I would need to be young again
And the glass now it is stained
The memories they fade away
And all that we attained
Gets older now each day
But the memory of our love
And although we are apart
Will simply have to be enough
To always keep you in my heart.

Keeping the faith!

The years have passed, my faith is strong
My voice still sings the same old song
The morning comes like a fresh new wave
To belong to God, yet not a slave
My heart is filled with praise for Thee
Sink or swim, my mind is free
But who can tell what tomorrow brings
And yet I know, my heart still sings
The day will come when I must go
It has been said – it shall be so
Now while on my life I reflect
I know I learned love and respect
Life is not easy, that's for sure
Belief in God helps to endure
And when one day you think of me
Remember now my soul is free!

Knowing

The sky is blue, the grass is green
The future it cannot be seen
But some say they can see it all
Just by looking into a crystal ball
They have with some notoriety
Managed to fool even high society
Personally, I don't want to know
I learn my future as I live and grow
Knowing would be like a kind of theft
Leaving no mystery to the life that's left

Lazybones

I managed now another day
With simply nothing on my mind
I did the same thing the other day
I think I'm trying to unwind
Same again tomorrow for I haven't finished yet.

Learning to love

There are times in our lives that will be filled with mistrust
Because when you are young, you feel jealousy, feel lust.
The burning sensation, of wanting to own the one you love,
You pray for reassurance, but not for guidance from above.
But when you grow older, you learn to trust, to love, to live,
And most importantly, you realise you have to give.
There might be times I might just take and not give enough
And I'm sure you'll sometimes wonder about me and our love.
The only certainty in life is that we must die one day
And it could be before I have had time to say:
That as sure as there are waves upon the sea,
I know that I love you and you love me.

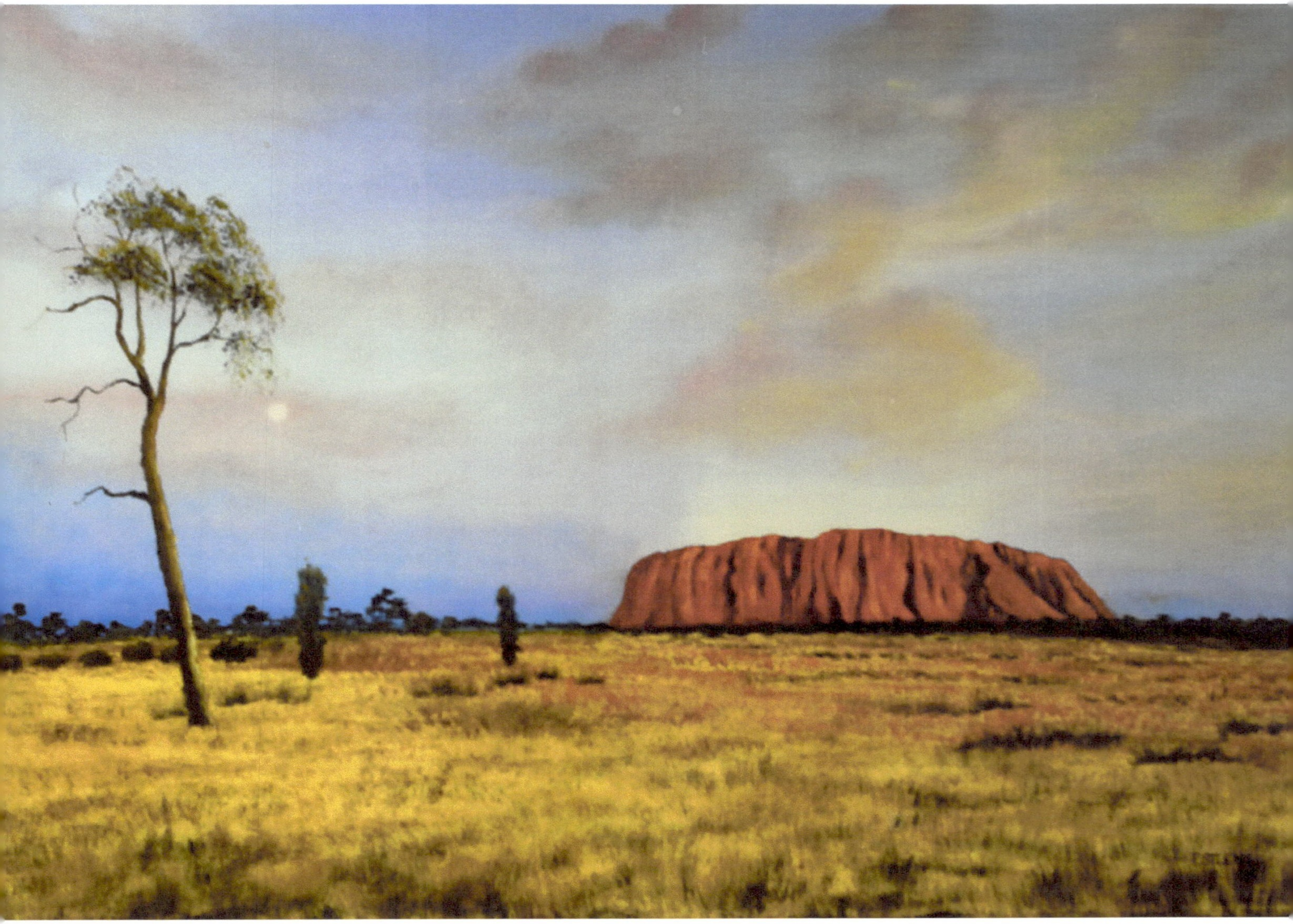

Dedicated to my mother-in-law.
Rest in peace, mum.

Legacy

For some 70 odd years of my life
I was a mother, grandmother, friend and wife.
But now that my life has been run
The life of others has just begun.
And while you all stand there and cry
I know it's time for me to leave and die.
So goodbye to all, family and friends
But this is how all life begins and ends.
And as I stand at Heavens doors
I ask "Let me in Lord, I am a child of yours".
You all know where I came from
But now you know that I am home.

Lemon tree oh so pretty

I'm so green and lush
Out in the soothing rain
And I can feel a rush
To my lemon scented brain.
Autumn now is cold and grey
Followed by the winter snow
My leaves are dry as hay
Perhaps get eaten by a cow.
But that's just a month or three
Followed again by the spring
After all I'm just a tree
And I will do my thing.
Now my leaves will grow
And I feel it once again
The joy and the glow
In my lemon scented brain.

Lest we forget

It seems like only yesterday
Our diggers we would praise
And with the image of that yesterday
Our children we would raise.
The diggers of the First World War
Gave their lives and died with pride
That pride doesn't live no more
Bureaucracy has pushed it aside.
Yes who remembers this war?
Who cares about a lone grave?
Yonder are a thousand more
Who cares that they were brave?
The future looks so dim and grey
And I say this with much regret
The dignity we mentioned when we pray
Has changed to – **It is best we forget**!

No Australian parliamentary representatives at the WWI site in France.

Let me....

Let me love, let me live, let me laugh, let me cry
Give me friends that help make this life go by
But until the day that I must surely die
Let me love, let me live, let me laugh and let me cry

Life

There is nothing at the end of a rainbow
There is neither silver or a pot of gold.
There is never really a new tomorrow
There is only a today that we should hold.
So why is life so different now?
Compared to when it first begun?
Gone forever is the afterglow
Of lullabies that we heard sung.
Memories of bygone days we treasure
As father time extends his wrinkled hand
And suddenly the things that we measure
Are in an hour glass that's filled with sand.
We watch it slowly falling, grain by grain
And like every being that ever lived
We wish we could have it all again,
Our childhood, our life, this precious gift!
Why is then as we grow old
We haven't learned from our mistakes
And realise that life itself is gold
Life is life, and finally, our life it takes.

Life as such

There's no need to sit and cry
Thinking you missed out on bliss
You get born and than you die
That's just the way it is!

Life in verses

The tears of love have stained the sky
The footsteps in the sand are gone
There is no point in asking why
For what is gone for sure is gone
Confess, confess its love you miss
The kindness of a gentle touch
The warmest lips, the sweetest kiss
Their absence is just too much
You can scream in pain and rage
While you feel the cold blade of the knife
And yet, and yet, it's just a page
In the book that we call life
But once that page has been read
And all the words have been spoken
There are feelings left that are unsaid
The memory of love, an unclaimed token

Life!

Life is not like the setting sun
That rises again in the morning
It can be sad, it can be fun
And it can end without a warning!

Life's highway

I'm a rolling stone trying to reach the top
Don't know the reason why it is my goal
I'm halfway there now and I can't stop
All I know is, it will save my soul
Travelled the lost highway for many years gone by
Hoping that you might call my name
But I guess that until the day that I die
Every bluebird's song, will always sound the same
Bitter tears have left a trail in the dust
Don't know if I'll ever reach that distant top
Golden dreams have ever so slowly turned to rust
And I know some day this rolling stone will stop
Come that day, the wind will whisper these words
You can't go on and you can never more look back
And you will know the saddest words ever heard
You have reached the end of the lost highway's track

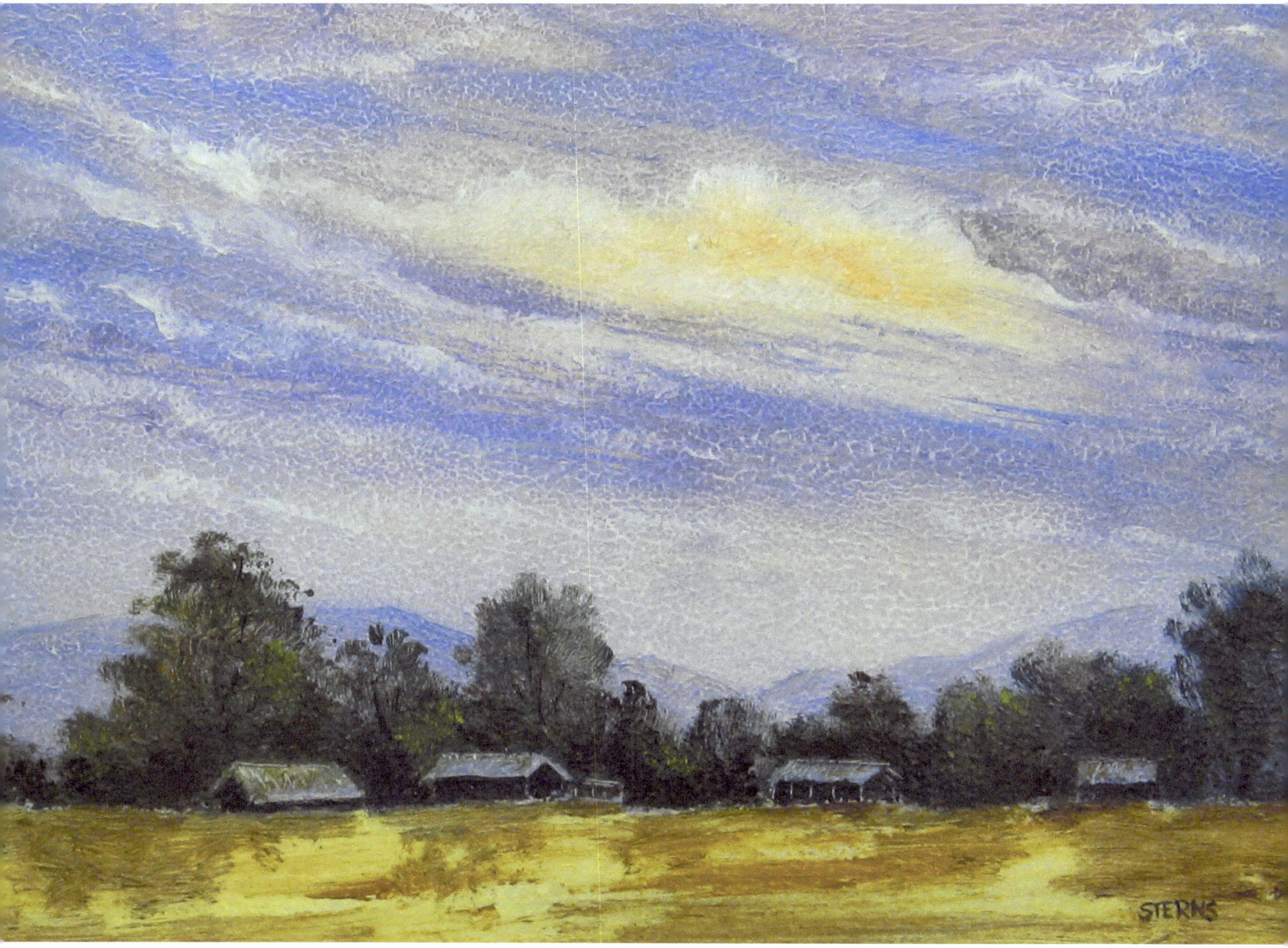
STERNS

Limbo

I'm standing on this ladder
Am I going up or going down
If I yell it doesn't matter
For there is no other sound
So am I going up to Heaven
Or going down to hell
At the age of ninety-seven
It is pretty hard to tell
I hold a cup with money in it
And I wear a dirty old gown
Was I a beggar or a winner
Do I smile or wear a frown
I don't seem to be moving
For I'm fixed here on this rung
Am I going where there's moaning
Or where praises will be sung
I think that the grim Reaper
Has left me here out in the cold
And forgot to tell the keeper
Because he too is getting old
So I'm standing on the brink
Waiting for someone to take my hand
And I really prefer to think
It's up to the promise land.

Limited choices

Heard a man say – what to do
Besides drinking and sniffing glue
Breaking, entering, stealing a car
Passing out in a dingy bar
Seems the options out there are few
What is a man really to do?

A little prayer

Oh Lord, I always tried to be
The husband and father I was meant to be.
But I am human, that is understood
And I did the best that I could.
Yet when I stumbled and couldn't see
I knew you were there for me.

And when I walked in deep despair
Oh Lord, you were always there.
So when I lay me down to sleep
I pray the Lord my soul to keep.
And should it be that I pass away,
I hope they find something nice to say.

Living it to the limit!

If you believe the things that you hear
And there are some stories I've been told
There will be nothing left of this earth, my dear
Nothing at all by the time we are old
So let us really live it up, sweetheart
Let's take that bull right by that horn
Let the devil think he's done his part
And let us watch him scream and scorn
Because if we can cheat the devil, dear
For he thinks he is really very smart
We've smoked it all, drank all his beer
And put the horse behind the cart!

Lonesome dove!

He looks at her, there on the ground
His mind just cannot comprehend
He listens hard but there's no sound
A moment in time – the End?
Where are you, where are you?
He calls down to his love
Cucuroo, cucuroo
The cry of a lonesome dove!

Looking back

When you're young, you want to be older,
You learn new moves, learn to be bolder.
You dream of a girl with golden hair,
But you soon know that life isn't fair.
You learn to laugh and you learn to cry,
You're in love, but you want to die.
And now another girl has come along,
You learn the words to a different song.
Life can be happiness, life can be pain,
And as you listen to the falling rain,
You know you have grown a bit older,
You know not to look back over your shoulder.
Live each day as if it's your last,
Don't dwell on what's in the past.
Learn that you can instead,
Remember the past, but always look ahead.

Looking ahead!

Sometimes I stare into the blue yonder
Other times I just sit here and sing my song
Sometimes I wish I was the deep thunder
And I could teach people what's right and what's wrong
But my heart knows I can do neither
I can't stop the rain from falling down
I can't tell mankind to love one another
But it sure would be nice to be shown
That the road we travel on our life's journey
Is not one where we live to settle a score
But one where we live and keep on learning
To accept one another without hatred or war!

Looking back

Where have all the cookies gone
And where is all the laughter
I can see the moon and the sun
But where is the happy ever after
Yes life is like a story book
About the laughter and the tears
But when you have a real good look
There were cookies, smiles and good years

Looking forward

Oh how we changed over the years
Once we had sugar and spice
Now we have grey hair and tears
And would trade it for anything nice
Our memories go back to happier times
When we were young and so free
When we carved our names in the rind
Of my fathers old apple tree
Now it seems we have nothing to gain
And the night times are much too cold
We are ravaged by aches and pain
I believe now we are too darn old
All we can look forward to is being sick
The good times have all passed us by
The two-step is three steps too quick
I think this is a good reason to cry
And we do that for anything that comes along
When we walk, we seem to loose our way
Yet we know the words to any old song
I guess we have known much happier days!

The Loser

Sometimes it's good to be a bird,
sometimes it's good to be on the ground.
Sometimes it's important to be heard,
at other times best not to make a sound.
You can soar like an eagle through the sky
or you can crawl around like a snake.
You can envy the eagle who is able to fly
or you can learn to give as well as to take.
The Lord gave us the ability to feel and to choose
between what is right and what is wrong.
There are always winners and those that must lose,
but in losing you can learn to be strong.
The wise loser, is the one who knows in his heart
that there is a lesson for him to be learned.
The teacher the Lord, showing him a new start,
that with believing, a new trust can be earned.
So if you feel like a loser, speak to the Lord
and devote to Him some of your time.
He knows your anguish, hears your every word,
it will change your life, it did mine.

Love lives

Its autumn, the seasons are passing
These words have a wonderful ring,
They say that time is a wasting,
And that time changes everything!
Its memories that I now have to cling to
And winter is following the fall,
And the pain is no longer so strong now
But it's the good times that I will recall!
Times when you were by my side, dear
When I heard you calling my name,
And at times I feel you are near
Yet things are no longer the same.
It's been quite a while since we've spoken
And each night when I say a prayer

I send you my love as a token
Of how I feel about you, my dear!
Time passes awfully quiet now
And each day when I am greeting the sun
There is one less hair on my brow
But I know that you are still the one.
I know that you can see me and hear
Up there in the Heavens above
And it's been more than a year
Yet my heart is still filled with love.
But now I will say goodnight, dear
If I could, I would drop you a line,
In my dreams I still hold you near
For our love crosses space and time!

Love's token!

When we say our love's forever
Some people think that's a crime
But I think "I'll love you forever"
Will transcend all space and time
And now the angels have spoken
Yet they didn't say a lot
But they all wore the same token
A little blue forget-me-not!

Luck

One day the devil sat beside me
When I was drinking beer
He said – today I can set you free
For I'm here to spread some cheer
I looked at him with bleary eyes
And I said – I'm from Kentucky
And although I think your words are wise
I still think that I am feeling lucky
My eyes they wandered down the street
Maybe a hundred feet or more
Then I tried to get to my feet
And staggered out that door
He said – listen here, good friend
Are you willing to play a game
That would bring you in the end
Your ruin or perhaps great fame
I looked at him the best I could
Because the world was spinning round
I say – hey man, I wish that I could
But I'm standing on solid ground
I don't need to play, to be a super star
And I might be drunk and from Kentucky
But I recognise just who you are
So go to hell because I'm more than lucky
You can't offer me, more than He has done
I was just celebrating being from Kentucky
So take your offer and forever be gone
Because I only need Him to be lucky.

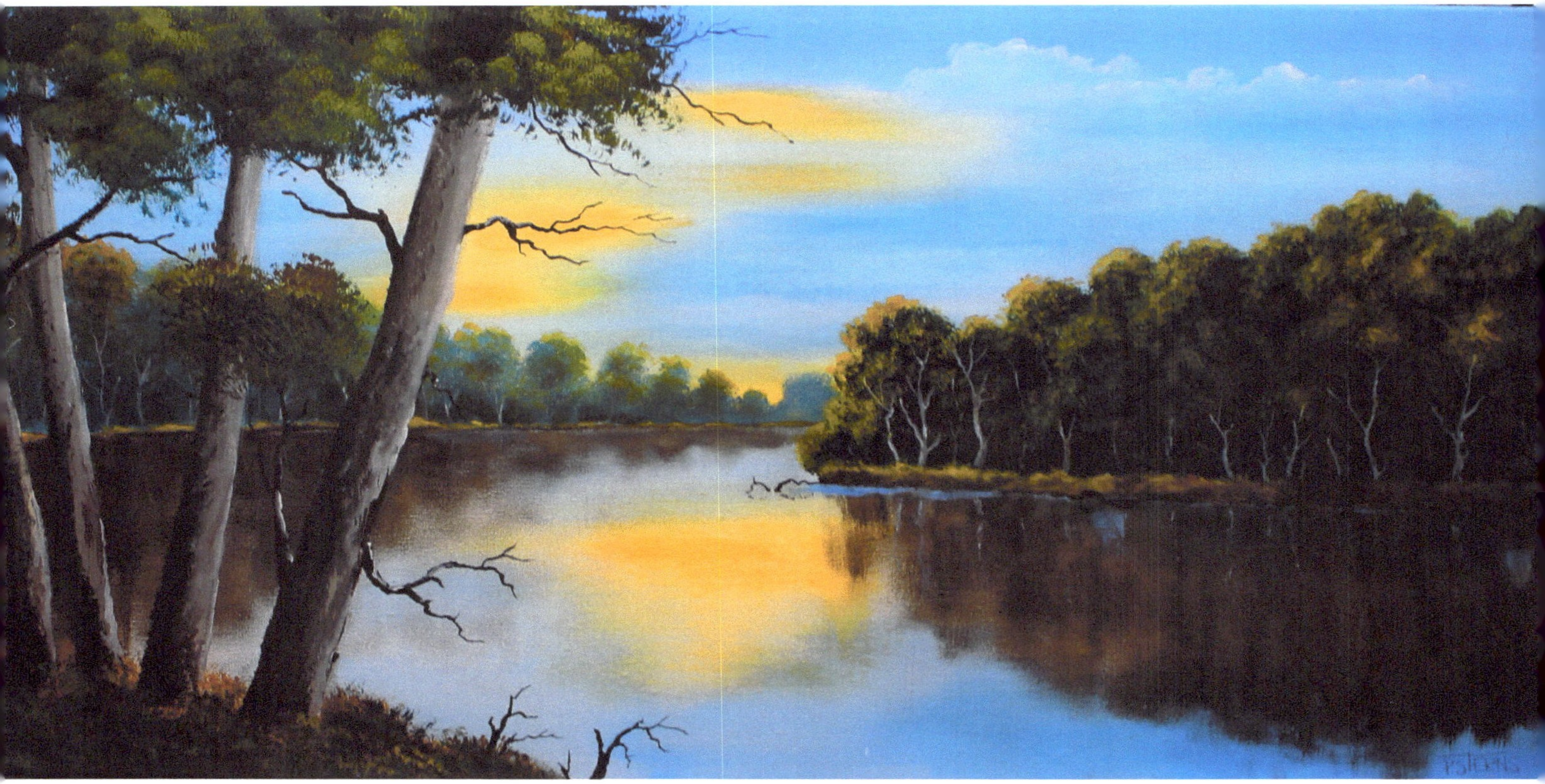

Make haste

I'm living in a different time
Where the singer sings no song
The sun rises but it doesn't shine
How I wonder what went wrong
People say that I am lying
Asking me just what I drink
When I say I saw angels flying
Only God knows what I think
Change your ways I advocate
Now the bad times are getting worse
Do it now before it's too late
And you're travelling in a hearse

Me!

When pigs fly up to the moon
I have thoughts of darkest gloom
Like the flower on the shelf
I miss me, my own sweet self.
I miss the night, the solitude
And the whiskey that is fortitude,
I know that I'm not really dead
For I hear noises in my head.
My thoughts are not worth a dime
If I don't get my 'quiet time'
The hardest thing, yet it's the best
The sound of silence when I rest!

Meaning of life

Who knows where I have been
Who can tell what I have seen
Who can say why we are here
What we love and what we fear
Perhaps it is someone else's dream

Measure of a man!

In the footprints of our past
Are the shadows we have cast,
Be they short or be they tall
Better to be there than not at all.
But a shadow is not a device
It can't speak or shoot the dice
Yet your live won't amount to much
If the two of you are out of touch.
You can be tall and arrow straight
And live as if life can't wait
You can be white, you can be tan
Neither shows the measure of a man.
If you are looking for the real you
There is no reflection in the dew
Don't look for footprints of the past
See what shadows you have cast!

Memories and time

The hands of time have moved
A decade or so at a time
The memories of love
Remind me you were mine
But memories of late
Are like a stolen kiss
And now it is my fate
That love is what I miss
The breeze might touch my hair
And whisper in my ear
That life is not that fair
For I can't hold you near
You will always be mine
Waiting at that distant shore
Till the hands of time
Can change the time no more

Memories of old

The years have come and they have gone and I am getting old
That much water under the bridge or so have I been told.
The winter's are cold, the summer's hot, out in the burning sun
And I'm a different man today then when I first begun!
Things remembered from long ago still fill my heart with pride
The snow man in front of the house, the sleigh rides in the night.
I recall those Christmas nights with my folks back home
Now I sit here by myself dreaming these dreams alone.
So many miles, so many years, the friends that I have known
The grand kids once so small and frail, are adults now, have grown.
Oh, how I wish that time stood still and I could live it all again
Instead all I have is memories and tears that fall like rain.
Memories, sweet memories, they come, they go and sometimes run
They don't want to understand me or the man that I have become.
For sometimes they are so unclear and others are frozen in time
But they can't take them away from me, they're mine, yes they are mine.

Midnight on the homestead

Moonlight shines across the land
Distant hills can still be seen
Silvery sheds silently stand
Where once a town has been
Nothing there but barren ground
The town folks long since gone
No laughter here, not a sound
I wonder what went wrong.

What next?
Union consultation fees?

Milk

It isn't due to industrial unrest
that our local milk is the best.
But we had this sudden revelation
that we pay for Union consultation.

They say it's always been their dream
to see we get the best milk and cream.
And, as long as the money flows their way,
it will stay like this, every day.

Missing you

Blow me a kiss
Touch me with sunshine
Tell me you miss
That you were once mine
Let a drop of rain
Touch my upturned face
Let it ease the pain
Be my saving grace

Mistaken identity

If I told you who I am
And just exactly how I feel
You would think I'm superman
The well respected man of steel
But I don't come from outer space
Or have superpowers I can spend
I'm a member of the human race
Who's simply named – Clark Kent

Old splendour large

Modern days!

The hustle and bustle of folk on the street
The murmur of voices, the echo of feet
The telephone chasers that last and last,
Can anyone tell me, did you get anywhere fast?

Modern times

The other day, the strangest sight
I saw a flock of penguins in full flight
But to me that's nothing new
I've seen a flying elephant or two
Next I heard a familiar ho-ho-ho
It was the red man we all know
Hey kiddo, I'm trying to do my best
But I'm giving the reindeer a little rest
Please tell the children not to frown
Santa is here; I won't let them down
So if you've seen a shooting star
That's just me in my new Tesla car

Mountain range

Dark clouds in the sky above
I hear the rolling thunder
My grandson's eyes so full of love
I look at him and wonder
Will life to him be hard or kind
Will he have someone to love
We can plan, but we will find
It's in the hands of God above!

My dog and I

He jumps up and puts his head on my lap
Looks at me with eyes that say
Let's you and I take us a nap
Like we do almost every day
I know that our days are numbered
I can tell by the way we walk, our gait
But for now, let us sit here and slumber
And I think for the moment – Heaven can wait

My mate!

How old do you think I am, he said
You see, I have travelled many a mile
Those wrinkles you see on my face and head
Were caused by millions of smiles
I don't know, I replied to him
Well, I guess you're at least twenty two
His face nearly split in half with a grin
You know, sport, I guess I like you too!
Well that was about twenty years ago
And we've been good friends ever since
His hair has turned white as snow
As it hangs down from under his hats brim
But my mate he passed away last week
And now my face it wears a deep frown
Then I look at the moons round face
And make believe it's my mate smiling down!

Mysteries

I make believe from time to time
That I no longer care
So I can tell this heart of mine
That you have gone from here
And it was a long time ago
An hundred years of course
When this foolish man
Gave his kingdom for a horse
So what distance must we travel
To find out what is the truth
And what mysteries will we unravel
Of our life and of our youth

A child looking at the war memorial's name plaques.

Names

A child in awe looks at the words
Of names and places he's never heard.
What do they mean, did they really die?
He wonders, as he looks up to the sky.
He sees a single rose, a wreath of laurel,
The countless names on the memorial wall
The bowed heads, a lonely bugle sound,
Heavy hearts, silent tears as memories abound.
In memory of loved ones, fathers and sons
We honour them, as if they were one.
Their names in plaques of bronze were set,
To always remember – lest we forget.

News flash on TV:

Students demand the right to kiss, smoke and swear in school.
They've been doing it for years.
I suppose it is easier if it is legal.

Necessities of life

When I hear the news it comes to mind
That my moral standards are way behind.
Student's demands are causing quite a storm
That kissing, smoking and swearing become the norm.
I guess it would cause those darlings wear and tear
If not allowed in school to kiss and to swear.
But does the discovery of a school yard kiss
Give a student suddenly understanding and bliss?
So when I hear all those student gripes
I wonder, are we raising guttersnipes?
If this is granted, what will they want next?
Perhaps it is the right to have classroom sex?
You might think I am sarcastic and cruel
You might even say I am a sentimental fool.
But why not go down the other track?
Learn honesty, understanding – and self-respect!

Never-ending love

I cry to the footsteps of your memory
As they echo in the empty space of time
I tried saying au revoir, even said goodbye
But no matter what, words have lost their shine
And summer now and fall have gone
The longing for your love keeps me awake
And when the stars and the night are gone
I find my heart still burning at the stake
When does it end this love I have for you
For it was forevermore, for eternity to last
I guess one day, when my life is through
An thousand years have come and passed

New direction

Would you believe me if I told you
That this life is second hand
And that one day when this life is through
You'll know I was a Christian Highway man
There were times I lived in darkness
When there was no light to be found
And I didn't have the awareness
Nor did I know who was the Devil's hound
For the good life that I was living
Whiskey and women and a good old song
For the feeling that it was giving
Was that the world just rolled along
But one day I had this great sensation
It happened just like a magic puff
And I came to the realisation
That I didn't need all that stuff
Somehow the good Lord took me hold
I don't know how it came about
I realised that I had been fooled
Into this life of the fast living crowd
And I know that I've been wrong
That I had stumbled along the way
And because I cannot sing a song
I say a prayer of thanks every day

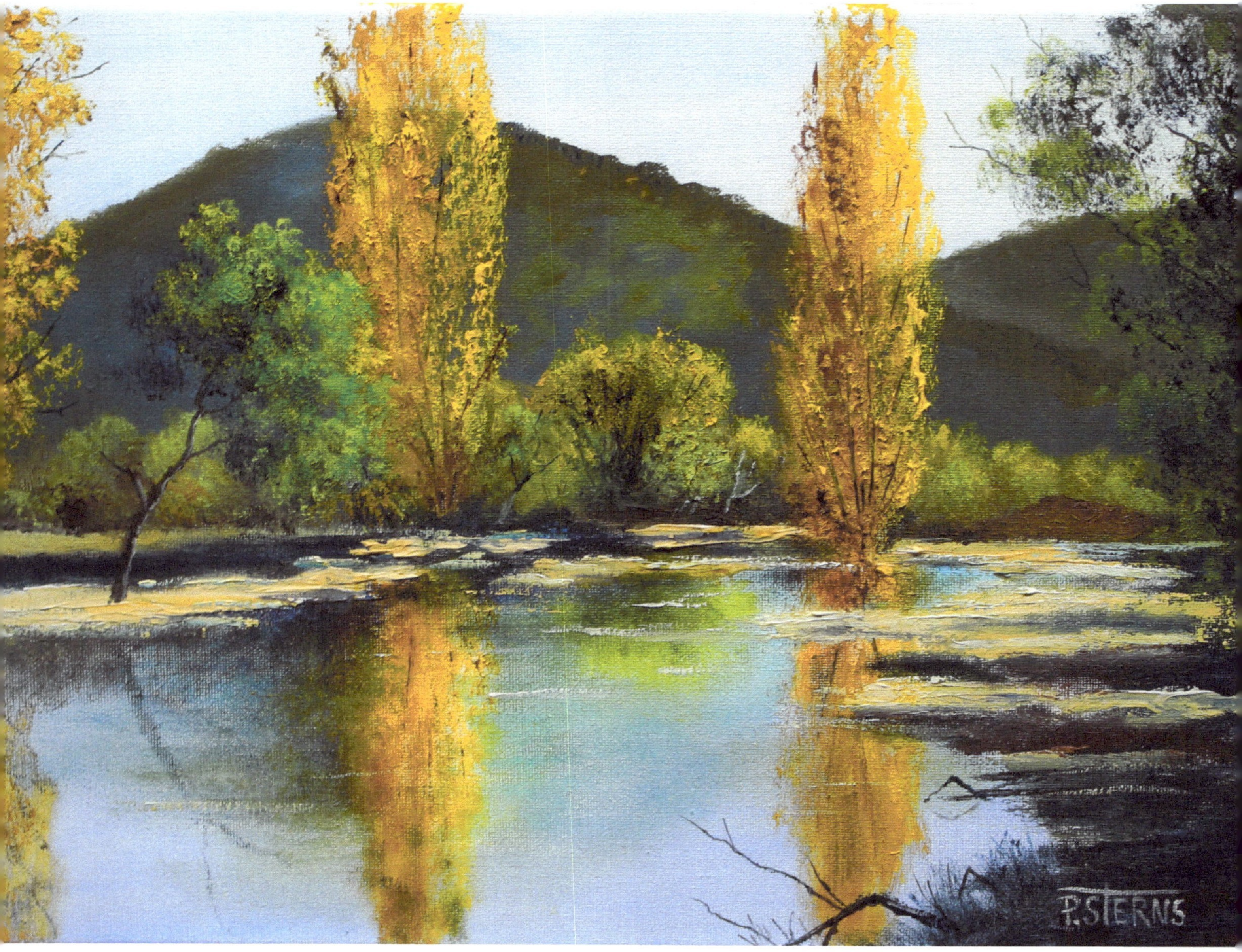
P.STERNS

New hope

When I was young I played in the snow
Heard a carol sung from long ago
I'm not sure if it was Silent Night
But I saw a star so distant yet so bright
My heart was filled with hope and love
As my spirit rose to the Heavens above
That moment gave me purpose in my life
But reality cut my dreams just like a knife
Don't let the dreams of yesterday die down
Keep them alive, smile, don't wear a frown
For the Lord above gave you His son
Despite of all the bad things we've done
Learn to live in hope and not in fear
And occasionally you can shed a tear
We have much that we can be thankful for
Before we cross to Jordan's distant shore

New hope

As I'm walking down this road
Wearing clothes, old and worn
My shoulders bent by my load
When I heard that Christ was born
Barely able to live, to cope
Torn by guilt and by strife
Those wondrous words gave me hope
Gave me heart and a new life
We all search for our salvation
And we hope that we will find
A way out of this damnation
Let us pray now for all mankind

New seasons

Six months have passed or maybe it's three
Where blossoms have been there's fruit on the tree
The seasons are passing and autumn is near
And memories are now all that I can hold dear
But memories they fade like the fog in the sun
Before you know it another winter has begun
When that is gone, spring will make a new start
And old memories again will awaken in your heart
So think of tomorrow as a new yesterday
It is a gift for which you don't have to pay
And when you reach the autumn of your years
Spend them with smiles and sometimes with tears
Memories will remind you of what once has been
Some will seem real but mostly like a dream
Be grateful for your life and the stars that shine
And give thanks to the Lord with a glass of sweet red wine

New wisdom

If every ending is a new beginning
Then I believe my journey has just begun

New Years wish!

May the New Year bring you pleasures
Far beyond your wildest dreams
May the clothes that you might measure
Never more burst at their seams
May the God of love keep smiling
On the wrinkles now on you face
May you bask in the sun that's shining
Full of dignity and grace
May the words that you are talking
Warm the hearts to whom you speak
May the mountain you are climbing
Be the highest one you seek
May the Lord extend His blessing
As He looks at you from up above
May the one that you are kissing
Always be the one you love!

News item!

The twelve o'clock news has repeated
That interest rates have retreated.
Now I think that has to be just crap
And I don't believe my advice inflated
When I say – watch where you step!

No help wanted

Nearly went to work the other day
Thought about it to pass the time
For no-one here would show the way
How to get to the welfare line
Everyone said that I'm no good
Staying in bed, sometimes till noon
Begging for money to buy food
And hoping to get rich real soon
But hold on, give me a chance
Being lazy is not really a crime
So I'll just wait till I advance
And they call me in the welfare line

No more

I'm sitting here and I'm thinking
I should move to a distant shore
Be alone and do my drinking
For you don't love me any more
Traced the footsteps in the dust
Still the same ones as before
Lost my beliefs and my trust
You don't love me any more
Come the morning, the sun will shine
On that far and distant shore
I'll forget that you were mine
For you don't love me any more

Noble knights!

I have this recurring dream, it's there almost every night
Don Quixote de la Muncha, he is such a dashing sight.
Whether riding across the plains or resting under a tree
But mostly he is fighting, bringing villains to their knees!
On other nights, two American champs, they do their bit
Of course I'm talking about Pancho and the Cisco Kid.
And every one of you knows of the tall masked stranger
Shoots silver bullets, goes by the name of the Lone Ranger!
But I'm hoping that in my next dream tomorrow
I can cross swords with de la Vega, also known as Zorro!
He's the one with black mask, the black horse and cape
Who brings to justice those that kill, pillage and rape.
And who is it that hasn't heard of the English fable
Of King Arthur and the Knights of the Round Table?
I can't wait for Merlin, Arthur's friend, the Magician
Some say he wasn't real, just someone's imagination.
They're all real to me and to think so, does no harm
They are my friends but most of all, comrades at arms.
Go to sleep and meet me in your dreams, I know you can
I'm sure you'll recognise me, no, I'm not the Spiderman!
You might have though I was a kid that learned to fight
No, I'm not a Ninja Turtle, boy that's an ugly sight!
You can see me jump a building in one single bound
I fly across the country, faster then the speed of sound.
I am so strong I can lift a tank, even swallow dynamite
But when I am near Kryptonite I can't put up much of a fight.
But if you want to rescue the world from coming to an end
Then call for me, I'll save you, for my name is Clark Kent!

Numbers

If two is company
And three is a crowd
Then four and five is nine
For crying out loud
But if you thought
There is more to it than that
Do me a favour
Keep it under your hat

NZ massacre

When I look up to the sky
I see no wisdom passing by
A man with guns and no regret
People injured and 49 dead
A heart that's black as coal
May God have mercy on his soul

Oh Donald

There is no collusion
There is no secret deal
Just the illusion
That you can shoot at will
But there are some specifics
That were watched by Trump
Like the last Olympics
To see how high, Mexicans can jump

Old and new

It's funny how we view the world
At 20, at 40 and then at 82
One minute it's full of young girls
And suddenly there is just you
We learned to fly and went to the moon
And have really, really fast cars
I heard them say that pretty soon
They will be living out there on Mars
Who can tell what we will see
Technology is constantly new
We are still tracing our family tree
And the woman who lived in a shoe
Sadly they say we have advanced
Yet we are still left out in the cold
Regardless what we do or we enhance
We will still die as we're getting old

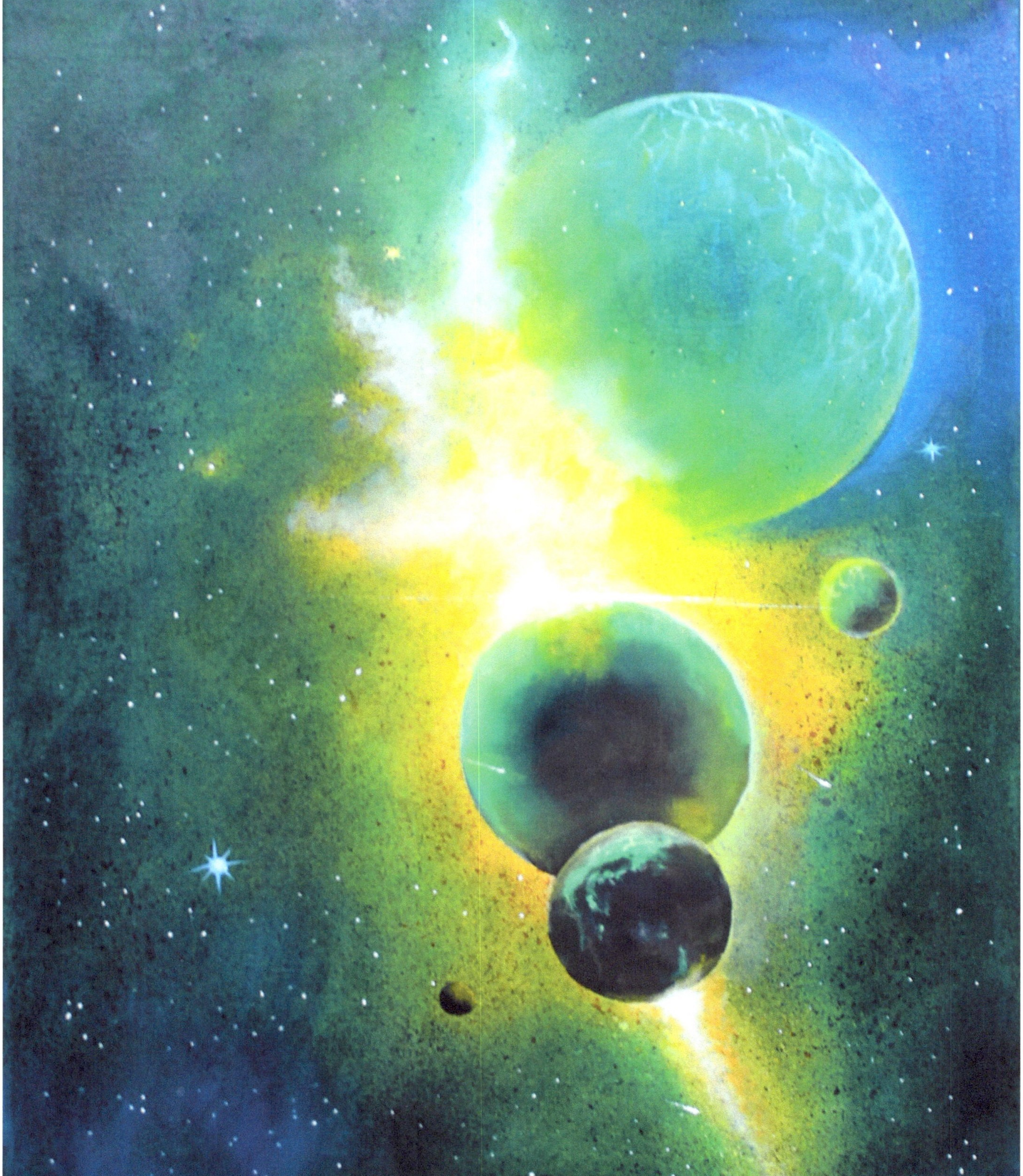
P.STERNS

Old memories

There's a little country church
Down a dusty old lane
Where my grandfather walked
Leaning on his trusty cane
He would pray and he would sing
While we kids played in the garden near
And we heard the church bells ring
With a sound so pure and clear
Oh so many year since have passed
And granddad has done so as well
Yet those memories still last
And I'm here the story to tell
But come the time that I must go
There'll be no mention of fame
I hope that my footprints will show
They led down that same dusty lane

Old tracks

The trail is gone that we once walked
Dust of the ages has covered the tracks
Time has erased the words we have talked
And there is just no way of turning it back
We had Bob Marley, Elvis and Martin Luther King
There was King Tut, Nero and Chief Geronimo
They would rule, raid and some would sing
But no-one ever had a six-pack to go
The traces of life, they have grown cold
Memories are dim, some even black
It's what it is, when you're getting old
And there's just no way of turning it back

Once a dictator

There are things to remember
There are things to forget
Like Christmas in December
And those moments of regret
If I was to tell you my story
It would take a thousand years
Just how I used to make you worry
And brought the world to tears

How I could never be the master
And would never sing your song
Everything would be a disaster
For it always turned out wrong
Who can tell what might have been
If I had had a different name
The whole world might have seen
Peace and freedom without shame

Once!

Once I had a father,
I was the apple of his eye,
And just like my mother
He sang me a lullaby.
Once we had big dreams
A house with a 100 rooms
Now to me it seems
It's great to see the moon.
Once she was a vision
So tall with jet black hair
Now the big excursion
Is a trip to Medicare!
Once I was a young man
With skin that was so fair
Now I'm glad I still can
Count the silver in my hair.
Once we had a love
That was greater than the sky
Now we find it's enough
To see the children play.
Once we had so many friends
It was a joy to be alive
This is how the story ends
Just me and my love, my wife!

One last time

There are moments long forgotten
In those dreams of yesteryear
They still appear now and then
And end up drowning in my beer
The clock it keeps on ticking
Shows neither pity or regret
And despite of what you're thinking
It doesn't care if you smile of fret
The wager that you made when young
When your heart was full of pride
Games were played, songs were sung
Without an aim or someone's guide
But all those now are bygone days
And it's time to say so-long
No time left to change your ways
Perhaps just for one more song

One man audience

He is a stand-up comic
Who is extremely proud
Watching a man drink a tonic
But never once laugh out loud
He's thinking, hell, what a tough crowd

Opposites

Once I was happy, oh how strange
Everything was so, so out of range
If misery loves to have company
Don't call anyone else, just call me
Give me heartache, give me pain
Hate the sunshine, love the rain
Give me misery, can't get enough
Give me anything, yes anything but love

Our blessings

There are the stars and the moon above
There is a thing called the Milky Way
But we have a thing that we call love
And I can feel it strongly every day
Sometimes it's known as a Rocky Road
Just because things don't go our way
Other times it's a lighter load
That we carry from day to day
But my blessings are the gentle kind
Here, not at some distant shore
They are the ties that really bind
And who could ever ask for more
Precious moments that we treasure
Oft compared with rings of gold
But you'll find you cannot measure
What you keep deep within your soul
Yet all the mem'ries we are keeping
Of happy days and of good friends
And of the times when we were weeping
Tell us that we're only here by chance
But if you think that I'm mistaken
And you don't really want to know
Could be the journey you have taken
Will lead you to somewhere down below
Where there is misery and constant pain
Each and every day another fall
Regretful tears that fall like rain
And not a single blessing ever more.

Our destiny

As the day is closing its eyes
And the night proclaims victory
There is a cloud preparing to cry
With the moon as guide to destiny
There are those who believe in the Lord
While others live a life of crime
Some will still die by the sword
It all seems a sign of the times
Let us pray for the life of our young
And hope that peace will prevail
So the words that roll off our tongue
Are not the winds of death in our sail
Cry you not for me, oh mother
There are no more songs to be sung
I shall be home with the Father
When my Earthly race has been run

Our future is what?

Now we pray for one more buck
Once we prayed our soul to keep
Now we hope that with some luck
We can text whilst in our sleep
We once wished upon a star
An aeroplane would us astound
Now we have a stretched out car
With music that is called "surround"
As I sit here now and reflect
The only thing that I can find
A society of greed and no respect
That has a dull and empty mind
God have pity on this world
Where drugs and money are our goal
When beauty is a tattooed girl
Lord have mercy on our soul!

Outback!

There is an old story of survival that just needs to be told
You are getting it for free although it's worth more then gold.
You see, it was years ago when Burke and Wills got lost
When they were about to give in, a kookaburra appeared as a ghost.
While they sat there dying in the shade of the old Coolabah
He told them they needed to catch and cook themselves a Galah.
He said it was part of the Australian Aboriginals history
But the preparation had always been a great mystery.
To cook the bird, he said was not going to be enough
For everyone in the outback knew the meat was very tough.
But for a bottle of whiskey he knew they carried in a box
He revealed the secret was, to boil the bird together with some rocks.
This was years ago and I'm sure that some of you have heard
That you eat the softened rocks and throw away the bird.
And to this day when a white man goes where the going is tough,
After a while you can be sure, you will hear a kookaburra laugh.
To all you he-man in your great big four-wheel drives
Heed these words if you really value your lives,
If the kookaburra's laugh you don't want to hear,
Stick to backyards, barbeques and an esky full of beer.

Pages of life

The tears of love have stained the sky
The footsteps in the sand are gone
There is no point in asking why
For what is gone is surely gone
Confess, confess, its love you miss
The kindness of a gentle touch
The warmest lips, the sweetest kiss
Their absence is just too much
You can scream in pain and rage
While you feel the cold blade of the knife
And yet, yes yet, it is just a page
In the book that we call our life
But once that page has been read
And all the words seem to be spoken
There are feeling left that were unsaid
The memory of love, an unclaimed token

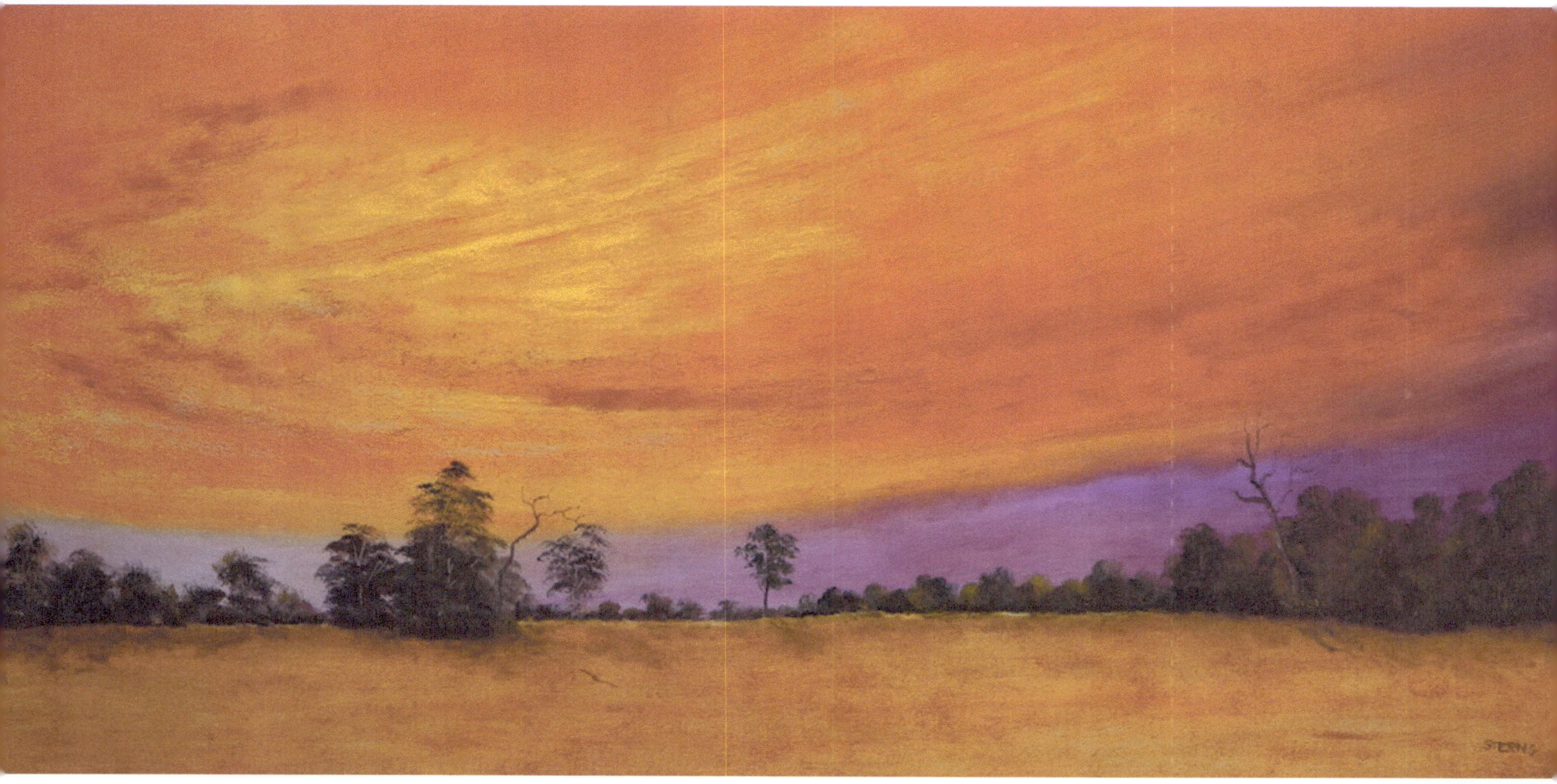

Passing through

Oh, the first ray of the mornings sunshine
The song of the lark in the blue sky
My heart knows that you're mine
And will be until we all must die
The dew on the green blades of grass
It sparkles like a diamond that's on fire
And it makes me wish that I was
There to touch your golden hair
I saw the rainbow at the end of a cloud
And I felt the cold touch of fear
And I heard myself saying out loud
How I wish that you were here
But what they say is so true
That no matter whom and what we love
This world is something we pass through
Until one day we will meet up above
The best we can do is keep our memories
Remember to live, to love and to hold
No matter sweet dreams or stormy seas
Treasure them as if they were gold
And if you happen to have some friends
Enjoy them and don't let them part
Tell them often before this life ends
That they always lived deep in your heart
Their friendship and the love you've been given
Welcome them all with your arms open wide
Tell them all that life is worth the living
With their memories and your love by your side
One day you'll know what's been said is true
That no matter whom and what we love
This world is only something we pass through
Until the day we all meet up above.

Peace of mind

Ask me not which way I'm going
Nor to tell you what I have seen
I don't know which wind is blowing
Be it further than I have been
It is up to the Lord's discretion
If I'm happy or if I'm blue
Sadly it's a very long procession
Where it ends, I wish I knew
For the ringing of the death knell
Has a soothing, definite appeal
But it's the murmur of the devil
Who is there your soul to steal
Ask you not for gold and riches
Lest it's evil you should find
Pray instead for something which is
Peace of the body and of the mind

Peace

I heard a song that is as old my tears
It seemed to come from heaven, way up in the sky
Did it come from where the roses bloom all year
I couldn't see, for the clouds were passing by
Perhaps if they moved a little bit slower
I would see the future and know what's in store
But there in the shadow of a tombstone as a cover
Lie all the memories of me and of my love
I do not dare to think of that what lies ahead
And it won't be silver and it won't be gold
It will be simple words I will say instead
I have come to be at peace within my soul.
I will always miss the love that I treasure
And on my own I will never be whole
But until we meet again in the distant future
I will be at peace within my soul.

Pearls

I will tell you by and by
Why I write the words I do
I have seen some people cry
At the taming of the shrew
But I found that was not enough
For clouds can fill the sky
I rather see that people laugh
Than hide their face and cry
I have seen the hardest man
Break his stare and smile
When that happens now and then
It makes my life worth while

Perhaps

When the wind rustles through the tree
Do your eyes like mine fill with tears
Do you wish we could be young and free
As summer ends and autumn nears
The tears they have blinded my sight
And the years have slowed my steps
But sometimes in the dark of night
I dream and sometimes think – perhaps

Perhaps you will be here with me
Once more touch my outstretched hand
When our souls meet, we'll be free
And then all will be well in the end
But until that day, I live in hope
And I do so from day to day
Slowly I am learning to cope
Believing that you'll show me the way

Pictures

Pictures of you are moments in time
When you used to laugh and to live
And for no reason or rhyme
The pictures that I have of you
Are the only thing left, life has to give

Pieces of love

Piece by piece and tear by tear
I say hello to my greatest fear
For I just found you're no longer here

We spoke of love, you said you cared
We named a star that we shared
Your love is gone but the star's still there

What caused the change, why did love die
It's dead and gone and I just cry
But there's no answer to the question – why?

Pieces of my heart!

She was a young woman of twenty three
Her life full of laughter and fun
What happened could not be foreseen
A man in a store with a gun.
She left before I could tell her
How much her love meant to me
My heart it feels shattered
Her memory just won't let me be!
The wind gently kisses the shore
Of the ocean of mem'ries before me
They are mem'ries I will adore
Till the Lord sets my soul free.
But today the sun shines bright
And my heart it is aglow
I think I will be alright
When I know where all the pieces go.

Pioneers

They cleared the land, cutting down the bush,
it was hard work, filled with pain,
some ran, when they heard of a gold rush,
but all fought droughts and flooding rains.
Most were sent out here for punishment,
others arrived with dreams of gold.
We remember them with sentiment,
those settlers, the pioneers of old.
We had some who became bushrangers,
the ones, that with society couldn't cope,
hunted by the law and total strangers,
to die from a bullet or a hangman's rope.
Some crossed the rivers and mountains steep
they built towns and farmed the land.
Others still, relied on wool and sheep
and made aboriginals their hired hands.
But as 200 years have passed
it has become a burning passion,
because now, in these modern days,
we're trying to become an independent nation.
Some will say, the pioneers of long ago
didn't struggle, fight and slave
to simply go along with the flow,
as for our own identity we crave.
Everyone's out to make their own luck,
people demand, no longer work and pray,
the bullock replaced by a motorised truck
I wonder what old Banjo would say?
Would he be harsh or would he be kind?
Lift his glass of ale and say : Cheers?
Would he say, that he did find,
that we are modern day pioneers?

Pot of gold

I don't know what I expected, but I can tell you now that I'm old
That no matter what books you have read or stories you been told,
A rainbow is just that, a rainbow that moves as you go along
And stories about leprechauns and pots of hidden gold are wrong.
Too many dreamers have ignored reality and found to their great shock
When they come to the end of their rainbow, they're lucky to find a rock.
The gold they have missed, is the love of a family and now to their great sorrow
They find that being old; it's now too late to face the world and a new tomorrow.

Precious moments

If I thought I had time to sing a song
I would write my own sweet words
It wouldn't have to be all that long
But the sweetest song that you ever heard
It would be the best song that's ever been
With words that sound just so sublime
I might have got a medal from the Queen
But bad luck mate, I just didn't have the time

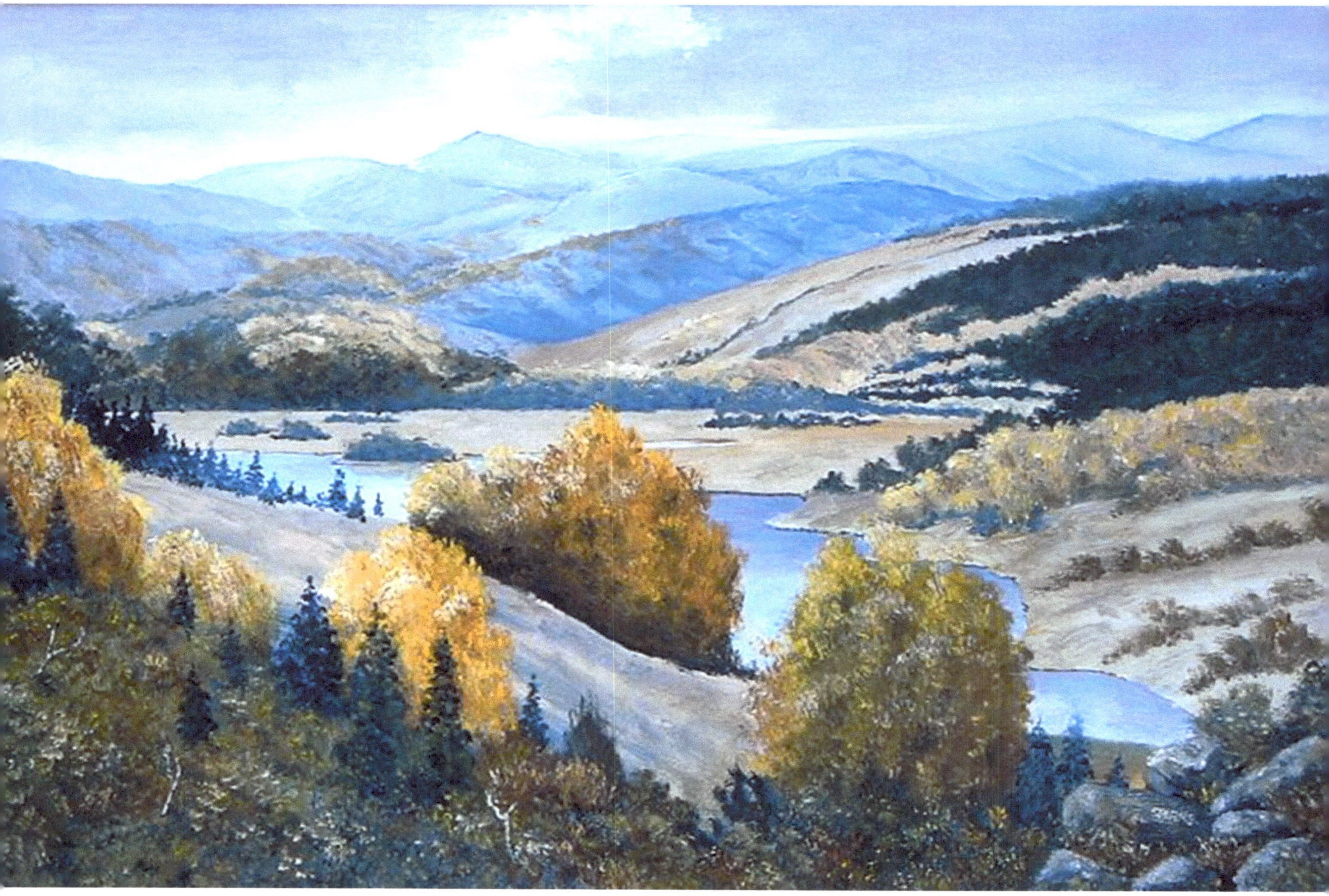

Sing along to the tune of Obladee obladaa, life goes on

Product names

I used Google and even Yahoo
To check on something called VIPOO
and I found this here URL link
The answer I found and I think
It covers something called VIPSTINK

Reality

Sometimes I think I sit on a mountain high
And one day I know, it will be time to die.
I remember things I have seen along the way
But how long has it been since yesterday?
When we are young, so proud and so aloof,
We think we are smart and bullet-proof.
We know nothing about tears and sorrow
And care even less about tomorrow
But when summer becomes winter and it is cold
I believe there is treasure in just growing old.
And understanding finally, dawns at last
That there is no turning back or changing the past.
Oh, I know it's been your wish and even mine
That we may slow down the hands of time.
There were sober moments and some that were wild,
Unforgettable ones like the laughter of a child.
And one day when the Grim Reaper I must face
I'll do so singing Amazing Grace.
But until than my life is neither empty nor bare
As long as I have dreams and memories to share.
It is called reality and such is life
It can be tender or cut you like a knife.
At times you are walking, others you drive a car,
But that's simply the way things are.

Reasons

My, my, my
A butterfly just kissed my feet
Cry, cry, cry
The river is getting ever so deep
Fly, fly, fly
Soar like an eagle up above
Try, try, try
But don't give your heart to love
Why, why, why
For it could leave you so alone
Die, die, die
Your heart has just turned to stone

Reflections of life!

For years I have searched and wondered
While I dug this dark and deepening hole
Sometimes I hear the roll of thunder
While the whiskey keeps burning my soul
In my dreams I have travelled all over
Sometimes felt the need for some love
But my heart is that of a rover
And one woman was never enough
At times life can be oh so lonely
Despite all the things you have seen
You wish for the one and the only
And dream of a life that might have been
Now Father Time and age are against you
And no matter how much you may yearn
Memories might leave you sad and blue
But what is gone can never return!

Regrets

Round and round and round it goes
The wheel of life it has no spokes
The wind it blows and can't be seen
You can't go back to where you've been
Memories are kept in an old sack
You carry when walking down life's track
Regrets are there, some old, some new
And the biggest one – the loss of you

Remembrance

I'm standing here at the grave
Of Jack Ryan, only 19 years old
He died fighting, trying to be brave
His life was worth more than gold
Every year we remember him
And all the others that died
It seems I hear the battle hymn
And my heart swells with pride
There is a day in November
And I say this with much regret
It is with honour that we remember
The ones that we cannot forget

Restrictions

Keep your distance, keep your distance
That is all we tend to hear
If that's the path of the great resistance
Why don't we get a mighty cheer
Can't do this, can't do that
Can't go out to drink and eat
Barely room to hang my hat
And even less to move my feet
Just how long will this go on
Is there hope or only fear
Are we meant to stay at home
For 3 months or perhaps a year
Now I am praying for my soul
Because life has become so rough
I feel like I'm living in a hole
And 2025 can't come soon enough
But in case you wonder why 2025
Well, I'm hoping this virus is gone
And there are some people still alive
For I don't want to live here alone

Rewards

At the end of our life's journey
Is there a reward that is due
For all that we are learning
And the friends that we once knew
I know that one day the Lord
Will give us our last call
And if He chooses, gives an award
So we shouldn't be asking at all
For the Lord knows that giving
Whether a reward or a fine
Is for the past, while living
We have added up over time!

Rhythm of life

Woke up this morning, feeling blue and low
Thinking to myself, is there somewhere I should go
Seems my plans and dreams, somehow have been sold
Or is it just a feeling that you get, when you get old
Since I was a young man, there were places in my dreams
Can't tell you where I'm going, but I know where I have been
The future now seems so vague and surely is uncertain
It is old Father Time with whom I am now flirting
He is smiling at me, daring me to take a chance
Perhaps I should up and do it and make it my last dance

Rich man, poor man

As soon as I buy one more round
I'll put the horse before the cart
I'll go to the lost and found
And pick up my broken heart
The poor man knows who he is
But the rich man knows the score
One will settle for a kiss
While the other still wants more

One knows he's the human kind
When he's got no ace left in the hole
But the other with his evil mind
Will even sell his mother's soul
Be careful what you wish for
To be rich might not be so great
Just because you know the score
You just never know your fate.

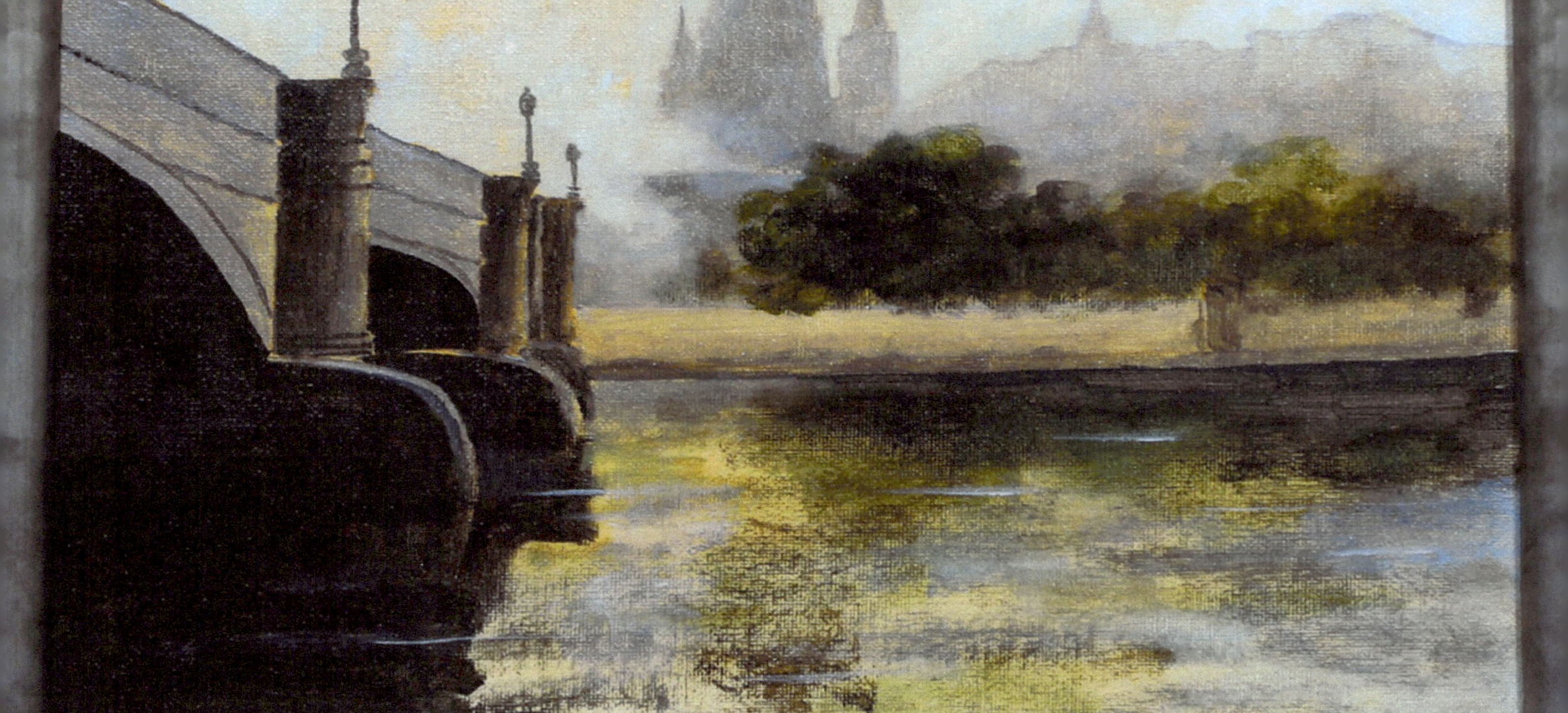
P.STERNS

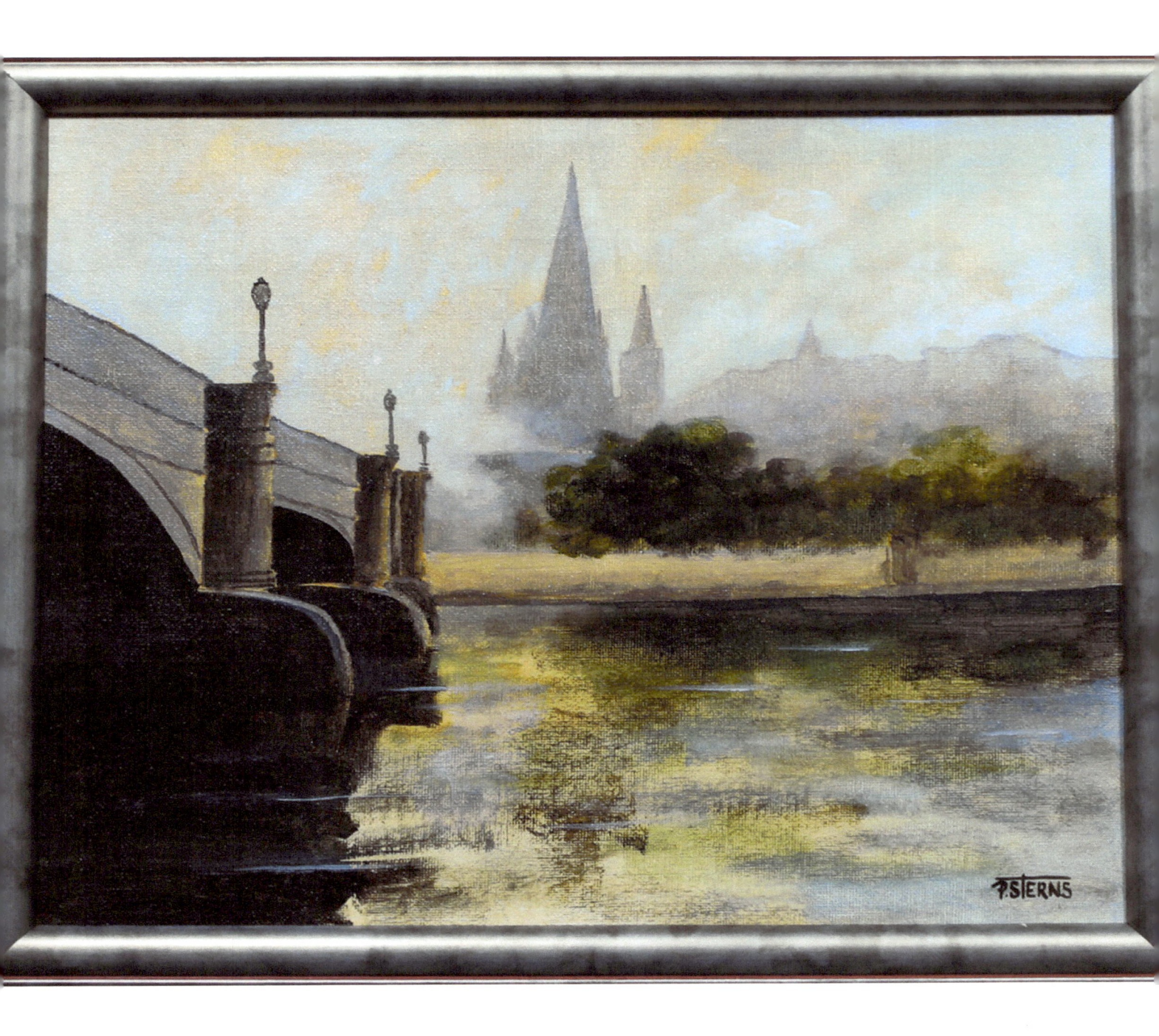

Riches

I feel the tears of the souls that have been crying
And I know the pain of the ones that are left behind
And every year the dead and almost dying
Do nothing to those that just pretend to be blind
Jesus spoke to us some two thousand years ago
Be truthful, be kind and turn the other cheek
But being written in the Bible doesn't make it so
If we are greedy and if our soul is much too weak
They say that salvation cannot be bought with gold
Despite all the fortunes we in our life have amassed
The only riches that will count, and so the Lord has told
Are the ones He's given us and He Himself has blessed!

River of time

Time is the river of life that carries all our dreams
And washes away our hopes and memories, or so it seems.
Time is like a melody you listen to and suddenly it stops
It's like the rain and snow, sometimes soft flakes or warm drops.

Time is like the seasons, spring like a new born baby's smile
The summer is our dreams and hopes that linger for a while.
And autumn is supposed to be like the reflection on a lake
But life and disappointments often prove that to be a fake.

And there is winter, oh yes winter with its cold and frosty bite
With aches and pains and crutches, even glasses to help your sight.
Yes time is like a river that flows silently and strong
And time is like a tune where we all get to sing along.

Yet time is like the seasons, it never will stand still
And what we make of life is mostly determined by God's will.
But life is short and years suddenly slip away like days
And we seem to measure our success on how much we get paid.

But father time is ruthless, can't be reasoned with or bought.
And it doesn't matter if we are lovers or as soldiers we have fought.
Generations lived and died, their bones now turned to dust
And in the end who really cares? And who will remember us?

Road of life

Today I went somewhere I thought I needed to be
Because I saw someone with familiar eyes
When I got there the only thing I managed to see
Was that life had handed me another pack of lies
I guess this can happen for it's not really a lie
When memories play tricks with your mind
You got to accept that it really was goodbye
And you're travelling on a road you already left behind.

Rodeo New Years wish

Now that this old year must end
I wish you all a happy New Year
And to all my rodeo friends
A friendly, bucking steer
And if you marry and take a bride
I wish you health and good luck
And let it be that your next ride
Is always more than an 8 second buck!

Suicide because of depression

Russian roulette

The spinning wheel, the spinning wheel
One chamber with one round
Is it joy or pain you now feel
Will you die without a sound
Now you spin the wheel again
You hope it will be quick
And will it now end the pain
But all you hear is – click
May God have mercy on my soul
When I'm standing at the Gate
Pray He takes me into the fold
Should that be my fate
And when the Lord speaks to me
And the angels sing with one voice
I hope my soul at last is free
For I think I had no choice

Sad truth

One day I know
That you will see
When your eyes are open wide
That your man is not your man
He's batting for the other side

Sadly

There's a memory that he clings to
From an almost forgotten time
But they say there is no antidote
For a feeble, crumbled mind
There are times he is in Heaven
But mostly he lives in hell
He's been like that since 67
And there's nothing he can tell
Yet once he was like you and me
With a kind and smiling face
Now his spirit yearns to be free
From dementia that took place

Sailing through life

Farewell my darling, farewell
Soon our journey will end
I remember the day we set sail
To go where the wind us would send
The years they quickly have flown
Just like the birds up on high
And now love is all that we own
And keep till the day that we die
So farewell my darling, farewell
There are no more sails we need mend
We have stories that we can tell
Until our journey together will end.

Salvation!

One night in a dream that was ever so clear
Angels were singing and a voice I could hear:
oh sinner repent, repent while you're livin'
And I will ensure your sins will be forgiven.

So there I was on my knees feeling ever so weak
While the tears of joy flowed down my cheek,
The voice in my head spoke of freedom untold
It was like the promise to Moses, the promise of old.

Oh, listen to me, your God from above
The one who gave you life, suffering and love
Trust in me and I promise you this
Believe in me and receive eternal bliss.

And when I awoke I was still in my bed,
The voice of the Lord still clear in my head.
So I lifted my eyes to look to the sky
My heart was so light, I thought it would fly.

For the sins of the world were washed from my soul
Suddenly the words of a song I seemed to recall
And a wave of love came all over me
For I, who had been blind, was able to see,

That we who are mortal and unable to tell
If we will rise to heaven or descend to hell,
Have only one life and before it does end
Must ask for forgiveness and learn to repent.

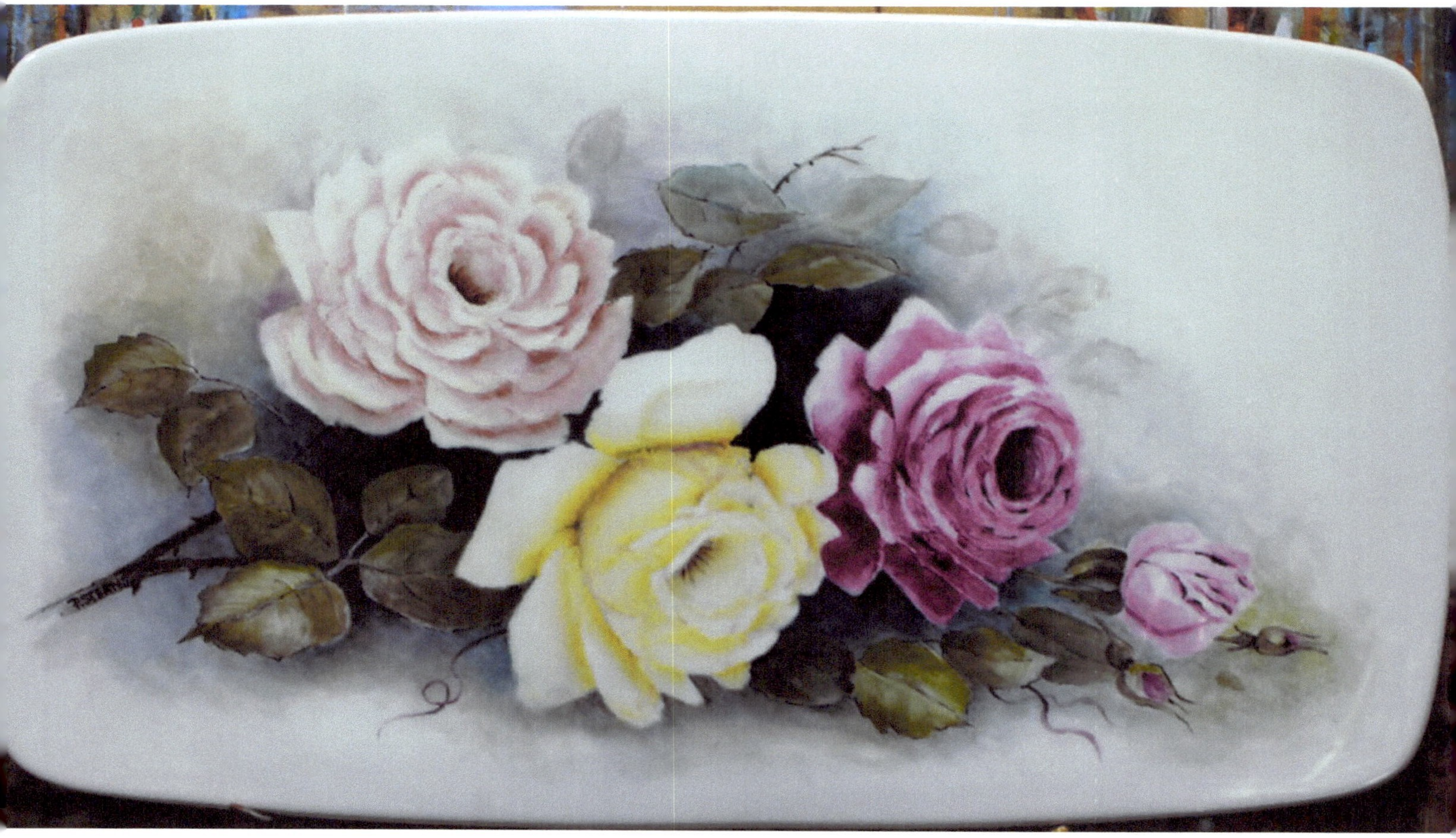

Scheming and dreaming!

There was a time when I was dreaming
I thought I played my cards just right
When I heard the devil scheming
Yet I thought I saw the light
How could I have been this careless
I guess it is not for me to say
Love touches you without much fairness
You think you can't live another day
Just as I thought that I was winning
In a game that's meant for fools
Than I heard the devil singing
"I have just changed all the rules"
When you think there's angels singing
Here in a dimly lighted room
It is just the doorbell ringing
Some good news about doom and gloom
And as I stare into my glass
My dim future I can see
Floating out there just past Mars
Pipedreams all, that will die with me!

Senior moments

I'm standing here and look around
What was it that I thought I'd found?
My wife looks at me with this grin
And makes me feel that forgetting is a sin.

Go to the shops and get some bread
Make a list in case you forget!
Me? Forget? I want to stand my ground
And I make the mistake and turn around.

She looks at me and I sense fear,
Now, who am I and what am I doing here?
I'm not old; there's still fire in the embers,
It isn't that I forget, I simply can't remember.

Serenity!

The little brook on the hill
Has become a waterfall
What was once a twig
A tree standing proud and tall
Far from the maddening crowd
The world here is so serene
I'm afraid to speak out loud
In case it's just a dream!

The servant

Hello father, mother, grandparents and brothers,
sisters, relatives, friends and others.
Here I am, who has since birth
lived, loved, worked and served on earth.

My life had purpose, love and a challenge or two,
and, since my passing, the challenges are new.
For it is true, the time has come,
that I now serve the Lord and His son.

Singing the blues

The dark clouds they are flying
Across the sky tonight
And I think my heart is dying
My baby's not in sight
Tonight I pray we'll never part
Because I'm the loving kind
There's one I love with all my heart
And one I left behind
But it's too hard to decide
Which I love the most
One welcomes me with open arms
And one thinks I am lost
Someone tell me if it's alright
If I sing the blues
Because by the end of the night
I will have to choose
The dark clouds they are flying
Across the sky tonight
And I think my heart is dying
My baby's not in sight
Oh Lord where do I start
What if I were to find
That the one that has my heart
Is the one I left behind.

Sinners

How often, how often, how often do we cry
When we know that in our life we've sinned
How often have we seen the bluebirds fly on by
And all our regrets blew away with the wind

There are tears that fall and stain our pillow
Tears that were caused by anguish and pain
We often compare them with a weeping willow
But come tomorrow we're all sinners again

We go to church and we have the best intentions
We bow our heads and we all kneel and pray
We ask to forgive sins that are too many to mention
And we go home and wait to sin another day

So how often, how often, how often do we cry
Will it be for all the years that we live
And will we keep asking until the day we die
Oh Lord, I'm a sinner and will you please forgive.

Inspiration – Katie Melua – Blowing in the wind

Skin deep!

Her beauty was something to behold
And it caused all men to stare
I think this story needs to be told
And all the facts laid bare
She grew up in a quiet little town
Far from the maddening crowd
But everyone's smiles turned to a frown
When the gossips had spoken out loud

For they said she got married
And was somebodies wife
And that the beauty she carried
Was enhance by the surgeons knife
She sported this beautiful décolletage
Something that made her real proud
And her newfound entourage
Would whistle and cheer out loud

Some thirty odd years now have passed
And what we sow we must reap
Despite our thoughts, nothing will last
And beauty is only skin deep
The years have wrinkled her lovely brow
When we are young we think we're clever
But that was than and this is now
And only silicon lasts forever!

Smoking grass

The scream that I hear is there in my mind
Along with the monkey who taught me to climb
I asked the monkey – tell me who am I
I'm here in a tree, do you think I can fly
He said to me – what gave you that idea
You see I'm no monkey, I'm just a deer
But I can see where you got this notion
For I'm standing on this wave, surfing the ocean
And that, I feel, might cause you duress
But a monkey that flies, couldn't do no less
So I must say – if it's weed you must smoke
You really should learn how to take a joke
Because if you should stop, you may find
That whatever you see, is just in your mind!

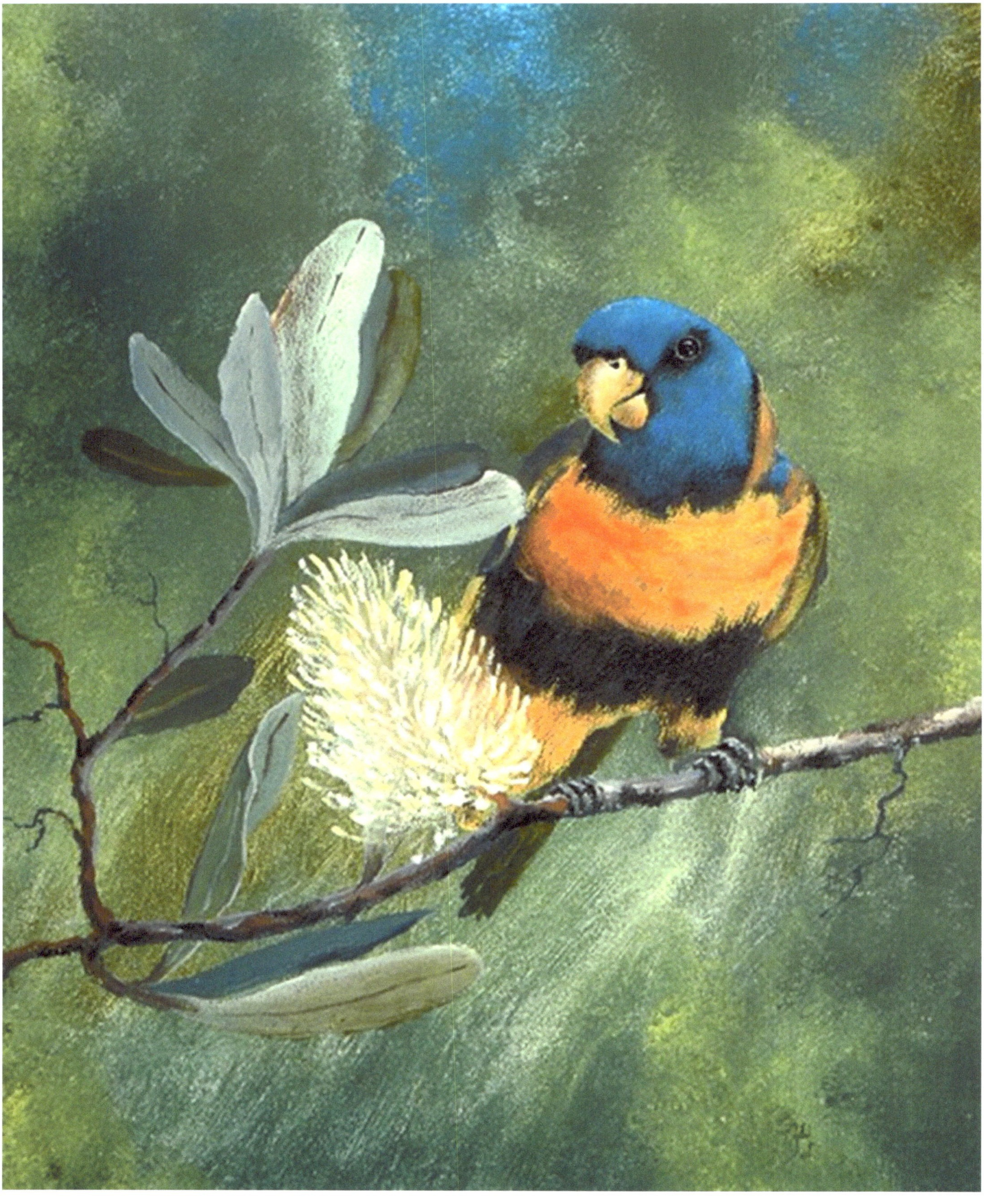

So sad!

Can you see the tears upon my face
They're not for the poor but for the rich
Who think their only saving grace
Is to know that life is such a bitch!

Some day

This old man sometimes sits
Under the old oak tree
Sometimes we exchange old wits
Talk about things we did see
Said he came from a distant land
Saw wars that can't be believed
Wore a star and a large black band
Lost a wife for which he still grieved
At times we just sit and stare
At other times we'd reminisce
Seldom we opened our hearts and dare
To recall the love we still miss
Sometimes I still see his wry smile
When I visit that bench under the tree
He is gone now and it's been a while
Perhaps now someone might talk to me

Song of life!

I listen now to life's refrain
About the dreams I did obtain
Some were like a shining star
Life's been good so far!

Political candidate is unable to give details of his policies or, if he has any. Confused? Who are you? What am I doing here? Anybody.

Son of Joh?

As a candidate you could say I'm vague
by the things that I have said,
but if I might be able to say so,
depending on which way the wind will blow
is where I am going to hang my hat,
and don't you all worry about that!

Stand tall!

It doesn't matter what we humans think
is fair and what is not,
we can sit and slink
or we can lay down and rot.
For the roads that lie before us
they have twists and they have turns,
but the desire deep within us
often smoulders, sometimes burns.
And the choices that we make,
as through this lonely life we go,
often sees our heart will break,
but from experience we'll grow.
In our minds we are giants
Trees, that are so very tall
but disappoints that we find
can never ever make us fall.

Storms

As the world greets me each morning
I know all that I can see will be great
It might not be all that I'm wanting
But it's better than finding that you're dead
The clouds may be grey but the sky is blue
Enjoy every moment that you're living
Because before you know your time is through
So don't waste your life, the only one you're given
Let the 4 winds blow from the east to the west
For soon Father Time says your number is up
You can look him in the eyes for you did your best
And only you know there were no storms in your cup.

Story time

The griffin is a mystic bird
From long forgotten times
The name these days is seldom heard
But in stories or some nursery rhymes
Perhaps Merlin had seen one or two
And some tall stories might be told
When they with dragons lived and flew
As wondrous beings they were to behold
But nursery rhymes are for the young
And yet for some grownups alike
There is a story that rolls off the tongue
About a kids finger in the dyke
So when we speak of fairy tales
And of Gods in Greek and Roman times
It all depends who the story tells
For some became favourites of mine

Street violence

We sing Silent Night, Holy Night
But oh Lord, what have we done
Praying as hard as we might
All that is holy seems to be gone
Just look at their ways and their faces
Raging and waving their arms with a knife
There is no compassion, there is no grace
Only the will to take someone's life
I see people fighting and yelling out loud
Screaming vile words of hate and abuse
Soon what were two turns into a crowd
And no one really can find an excuse
They say it's something inherent in us
And that to me is a real worry
It's like throwing someone under a bus
But never once to say that you're sorry
The fights that ensue like Blitzen and Donner
It isn't that I agree and don't want to protect
I find the principles of respect and of honour
Is something the youth of today seem to reject
What I see every day is so underhand
The behaviour more like that of an ape
So until all this mess I can understand
I'll just watch and let you – peel me a grape

Stupidity at large

I am protesting, won't stay at home
For I am a human not a garden gnome
These stupid laws are such a disgrace
That's why I spit and punch cops in the face
They speak of a virus that kills every day
Most of them are old and really quite grey
So now I'm sitting in this comfortable jail
And I'm hoping that someone will post my bail
I'm not complaining, I won't even gripe
For I know this virus is just a news item hype
You can't believe the stories that you have read
At least not till you find me dead in my bed
In the meantime I will go out and protest
Because I am smart, well, an idiot at best

A true story

The groom had proof of his bride's infidelity
and decided to take the ultimate revenge
by destroying her reputation in front of all that knew her.

Style

Here is a story, if I may be so bold,
About a wedding, that to me was told.
After the party the groom thanked his guests
And to put the bride's parents mind at rest,

He had pictures of the best man and the bride
Having more then a bit on the side.
The groom admitted that a wife he had lost
But to her parents it was a $32,000 cost.

And 300 friends, guests and relations
Now knew about the bride's so called reputation.
People often reply in friendly banter,
What's good for the goose is good for the gander.

It isn't always so and far from the truth
To say: an eye for an eye, a tooth for a tooth.
On the Lord's face I can see a gentle smile
For this was revenge that really had style.

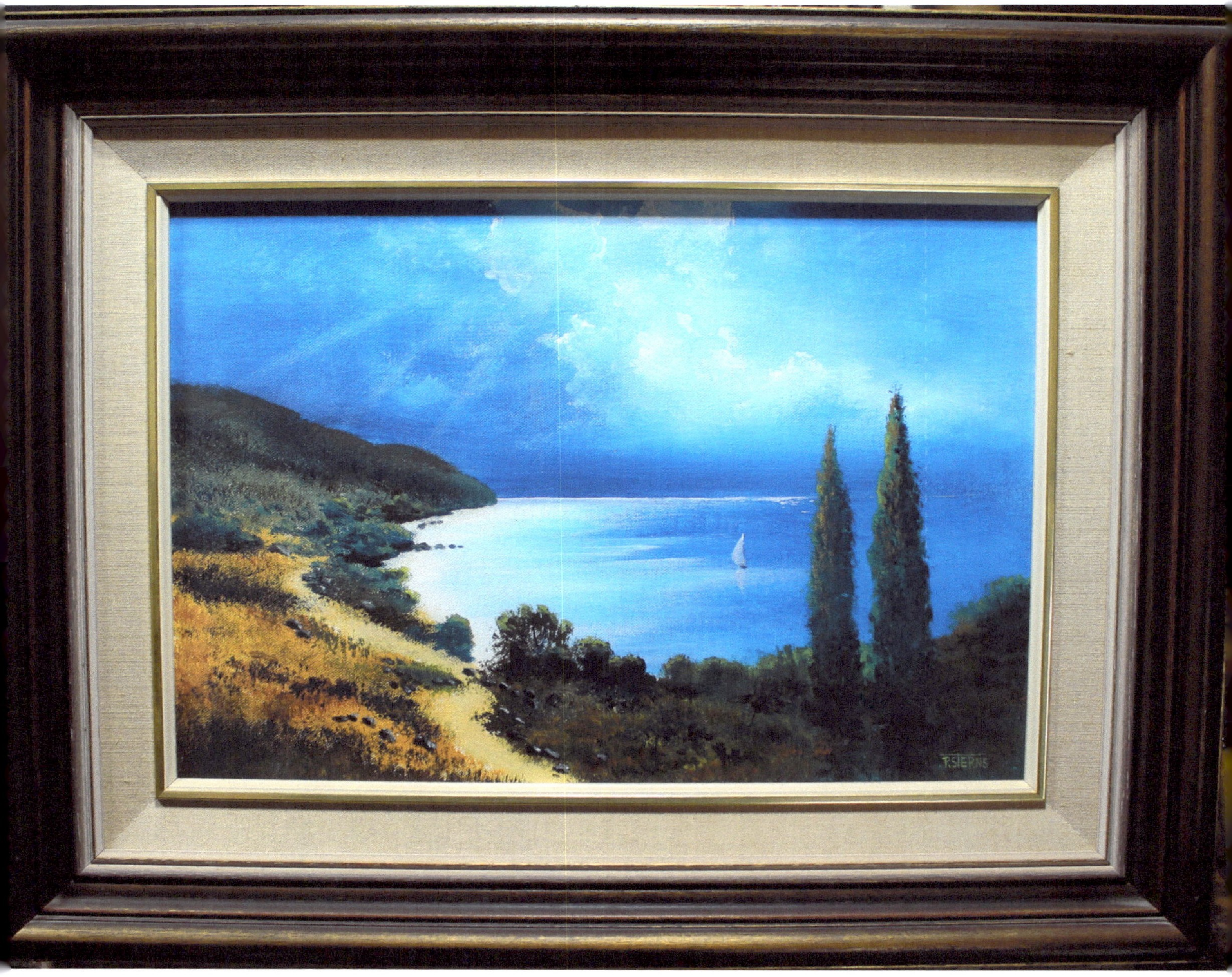

Such is life

When I'm trying to hold it together
There are more clouds than there is sun
They tend to call it stormy weather
And it's been there since you are gone
There are times that I want to share
But years pass like one, two, and three
When I close my eyes you are there
Even if it's only in my memory
And now I make a confession
Through the years that you were my wife
You held my heart in your possession
Which was the mystery tour of life

Suicide bombers

Another mother now is crying
And his father's full of hate
People just keep on dying
And it has nothing to do with faith
Is the world now free without you
Is the world now free of sin
Who is there that might have doubted
Who you were and where you've been
The world just keeps on spinning
And the gulf is deep and wide
Who can say who is winning
All depends on who's on the other side!

Sundown

Speak softly now since my heart feels the pain
I'm crying still, but only in the rain
They said in days of old
So I've been told
That someday we will meet again
But that could be oh so many years from now
And I have to survive those days somehow
Will I still sit and cry
Will someone say goodbye
And perhaps kiss my aged brow
These are word that I hear in my head
They are words that never have been said
I hear them now and then
When I listen to the falling rain
And they will sleep with me when I'm finally dead

Sundown!

The sun is going down my friend
And the moon is standing by
There are stars blinking up above
And no one wonders why

And once the sun has set
There will be the pale moon light
And all that's left for me to say
Is good night my friend, good night!

Surprise

As I woke one morning, my sweetheart by my side
The birds were singing the sun was shining bright.
Feeling like a cigarette, I found there was a catch
I didn't have a lighter or a single match.

Darling can you help me; I'm dying for a smoke?
When my eyes fell on a picture of this bloke.
There are matches in the drawer next to the bed,
I found them and lit my cigarette.

Now I'm wondering about the picture so in the end
I ask her – is that your husband or an old friend?
Nibbling my ear with consuming passion,
She confesses – that's me – before the operation!

Take a chance!

You never know how things will end
When you meet somebody new
Could it be they are heaven sent
Or cause your heart to be blue?
In modern days the road of life
It has potholes everywhere
And you think that if you take a wife
It is love or just a dare!
There is no guarantee to it
Nor a refund if you should fail

And when it comes right down to it
It's either heads or it is tails!
Life is not at all as kind
As the poets tend to write about
All those words about love is blind
I think their heads are in the clouds!
But if you do not take a chance
Soon enough your life is through
You've dreamt about a fine romance
But led a life that is cold and blue!

Taking aim

The clock has now struck seven
I have not yet moved
And now it is eleven
I'm getting in the groove
I shall be eight zero
But I say what the heck
I'm my own greatest hero
Eating scrambled eggs with speck
But just in case you wondered
And much to my own delight
I got the big one hundred
Firmly in my sights.

Talk

Money talks it's what they always say
Someone even told me right to my face
And it won't buy you happiness no matter what you pay
But I replied – you're shopping at the wrong place

Tall stories

It's getting dark and the stars they will shine
And granddad tells stories and is drinking his wine
He tells us of knights and kingdoms of old
Of pirates with beards and ships full of gold
He told us of dragons, of knights on their steeds
Of Merlin and magic and of some great deeds
Of Vikings and Odin who lives in the sky
Of heroes that fight without asking why
He speaks of Pharaohs and pyramids in the sand
And knows all the stories that don't have an end
But bridges must fall and dreams they will die
And grandma says granddad won't eat humble pie
For the stories he tells that make our eyes shine
Are all found at the bottom of a glass of red wine
But we don't care; we'll beg, steal or borrow
And wait for the next one he'll tell us tomorrow
When in the evening after dinner he'll call us all
To tell us stories of kings and castles so tall.

Teddy

I lost my little teddy bear,
he is all amiss,
I've looked here and there and everywhere,
he needs a little kiss.

I miss my little teddy bear,
his name is Humpty-Doo,
I think it gave him a big scare,
and he only has one shoe.

So if you find my teddy bear,
don't even wait a little while,
call me before I shed a tear,
because when he is back, I'll smile.

Terms

Today I saw a pachyderm
Who I really thought was you
But then I thought about the term
And I knew you were a shrew
But how can I be certain
When I really do not know
It's with words that I am flirtin'
And I don't care anyhow!

The Air disaster

A Cesna crashed in Dublin, what a tragic sight.
Sixteen people were on board and sixteen people died.
The crash site was a church, right there on the mount
And it's 269 bodies so far they dug up or found.

Now I think counting shouldn't be in haste
For it's time and effort they could waste.
Make sure to check the manifest lest you find
You dug up the whole grave yard but left one behind.

The albatross

They say that an albatross
Can fly for some 90 days
But what if he came across
Something that's in his way
Does that mean he'll fly around
Search for a passage he might take
Or does he land on higher ground
For suddenly he is awake
If I had flown for 90 days
And I know that's not my thing
Could it be that in many ways
I'd be known as a bird that's on the wing
But 90 days, I ask you
Could that be the truth
Or is it what someone knew
As the fantasy of youth
So tell me what will you do
To mend your wicked ways
Because before you know your life is through
And it's been just 90 more days!

The Aussie look!

I lie here in bed and my wife's stopped snoring
It is time to listen to Macka on Sunday morning
But the other day I really felt so appalled
When someone said he didn't look like an Aussie at all.

I am an Aussie – not by birth but by choice
All that we stand for and speak with one voice
I love this harsh land that is girthed by the sea
How could he say – you don't look like an Aussie to me?

Explain yourself and I think that you must
Does he need to have a beard that is full of dust?
Tell us listeners; tell us now one and all
Perhaps he needs to stand about seven feet tall?

If it's true that from many lands we came
We'd be bright eyed, bushy tailed and all look the same.
But I think you were joking, it sounded like it to me
Because Macka is as Aussie as an Aussie can be!

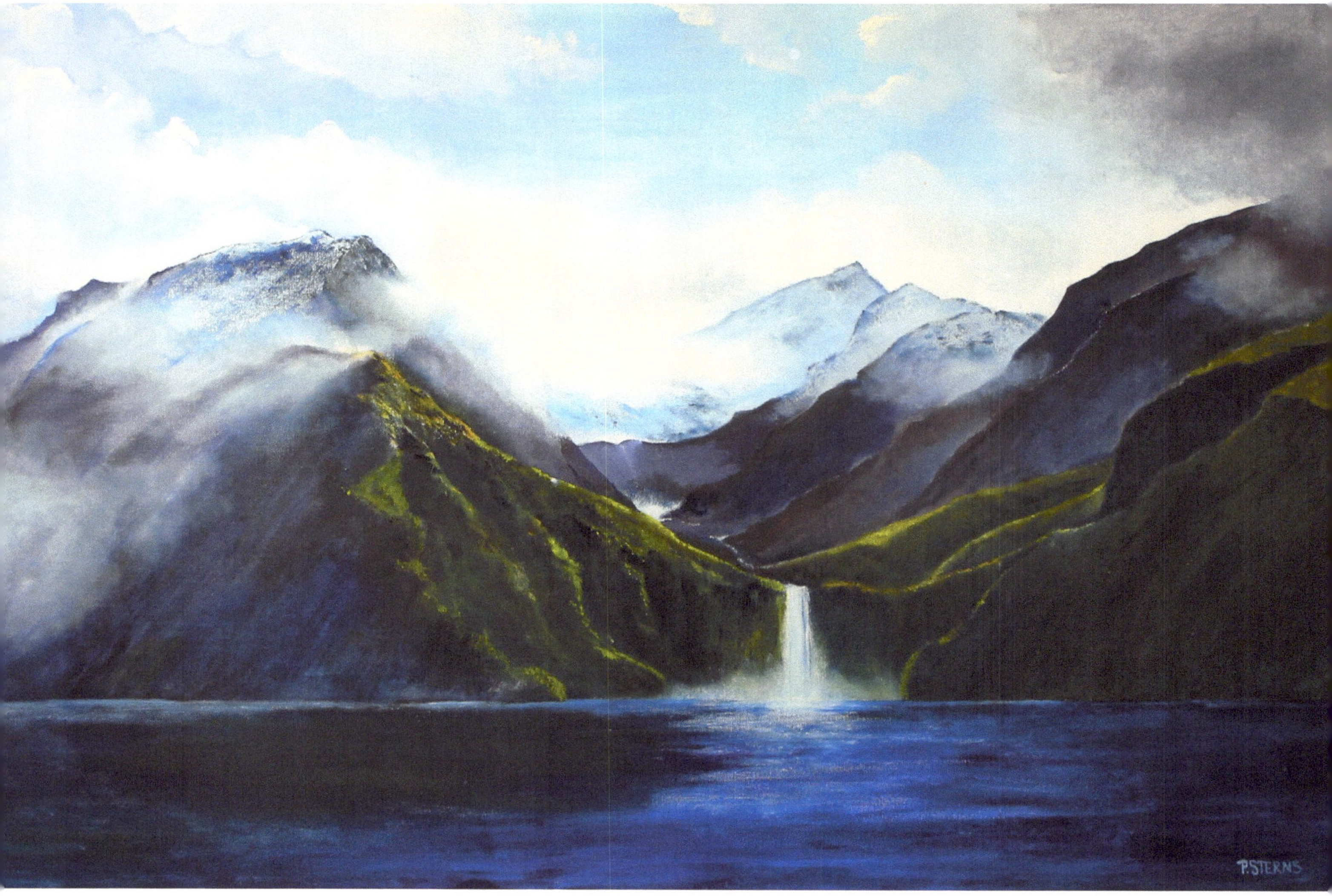
P.STERNS

The Aussie spirit

A farmer looks at his house on the hill
Turns pointing at the land all around
Seems it was the Almighty's will
That it hasn't also burned to the ground
Properties everywhere have been lost
Families with vacant eyes stand and stare
People have lost their lives, oh what a cost
Devastation that is almost too hard to bear
But they are Aussies, yes, that's their name
Battlers and fighters who are ready to start
Fighting fires and floods, all part of the game
And that's why we are known for our heart

The Bible

Who can hear the word of God
Who knows that His child is born
Who knows that on this earth He trod
And that the crown of thorns He's worn
Who knows what pain was in store
And that all the sins from us He took
So that we can live forever more
But if you don't, just read His book

The big match

I had someone tell me
That even losers can win
You don't have to be fancy
Just lead with your chin
It need not be Friday
And it need not be now
But if it's a Tuesday
We'll go and put on a show
I'll come out singing
Right after my lunch
You'll come out swinging
And throw the very first punch

I could almost feel that
You see we're never that rough
And when I lost my hat
That was good for a laugh
Now the crowd started roaring
Some even managed to cheer
But it started to get boring
So we up and went for a beer
Now I sit here, I'm asking
Is it a rematch you seek
Because in glory I'm basking
Ok, make it Tuesday next week.

The big sleep!

The years they have passed
One day at a time
Life doesn't last
Yet we wonder why
Grey days ahead
Where once the sun shone
Here he lies dead
Someone's favorite son
A grave cold and deep
Described as a hole
It's called the big sleep
But where is the soul
The years they go by
Does anyone care?
Sometimes we cry
Is that Vanity Fair
No man is an island
Or an ocean too deep
Come take my hand
Lest forever you weep
The Lord he has spoken
His word He will keep
One day to be woken
From that big sleep!

The blame game

There is no confusion, there is no mistake
But the thought of a virus, keeps me awake
How long will it last while we sit here and wait
Are we all bound to die or will it abate
They are simple questions, but who can say
2 weeks at home or forever and a day
I am confused as to who we should blame
Some are bemused but won't mention a name
So tell me, oh tell me, you miserable lot
Who shall be spared and who shall be shot

The blessing

I have had a blessing
And it grows and grows
I'm sure that I'm not guessing
That no-one else about it knows
I have had a blessing
And it's more than just my sight
For I am here attesting
That I have seen the light

The blessing!

Take comfort in waiting
For the world to arise
The birds they are singing
And the eagle he flies
Should God speak to you
Take heed of the words
These are blessings upon you
The best ever heard!

The chase

They say that the grass is much greener
If we just climb over that fence
But I find that mustard could be much keener
If it cost just a Dollar and twenty-five cents
Why are we chasing the uncertain lot
Is it the nature of the human being
We should be happy with all that we got
And not worship that what we haven't seen
There's those that have, those that have not
Some even confess that they have sinned
But most of them say it has been their lot
To live and to always just chase the wind

The circle of life

She often spoke about God's children
Never mentioned Mickey Mouse
Always said one day, God willing
We shall all live in His house
She's been gone now for many years
I believe it's nigh on forty some
Dad and I we shed our tears
She had left us an empty home
And dad himself since passed away
So did my own sweet, loving wife
I'll follow their footsteps one day
Such is His will, yes, such is our life

The circle

I never knew how empty this world can be
But I found out the day that you left me
A shooting star was leaving its mark in the night
To some it is a demon but to most a welcome sight
Some tend to think that life is a bother
But if nothing else, learn to be kind to one another
And I hope when the tears have dried on my face
That someone at my grave will sing Amazing Grace
Because I know when my last breath releases my soul
My birth and now my death will make this circle whole.

The classics

Opera is not everyone's thing
The word alone, an ominous ring
Verdi said – you reap what you sow
Hence the opera – if she wriggles, let go

The conclusion

As my life slowly drifts away
I live it now from day to day
I'm deep in thought
As to what life has brought
Found what has past, you can't take away

The convert!

A bearded man with a gun
Which he held to my head
Said – become a believer in the ONE
Or believe me you'll be dead
So you my might call me a chicken
Or say that I've got no drive
But chicken is finger lickin'
And I want to be alive
It wasn't so much out of shame
But for reasons of my health
That I took on a brand new name
Just call me – Aisheed Miseff.
And as I sit up here and ponder
About the strange name I have
It's better to look into the yonder
Then be lying in a lonesome grave....

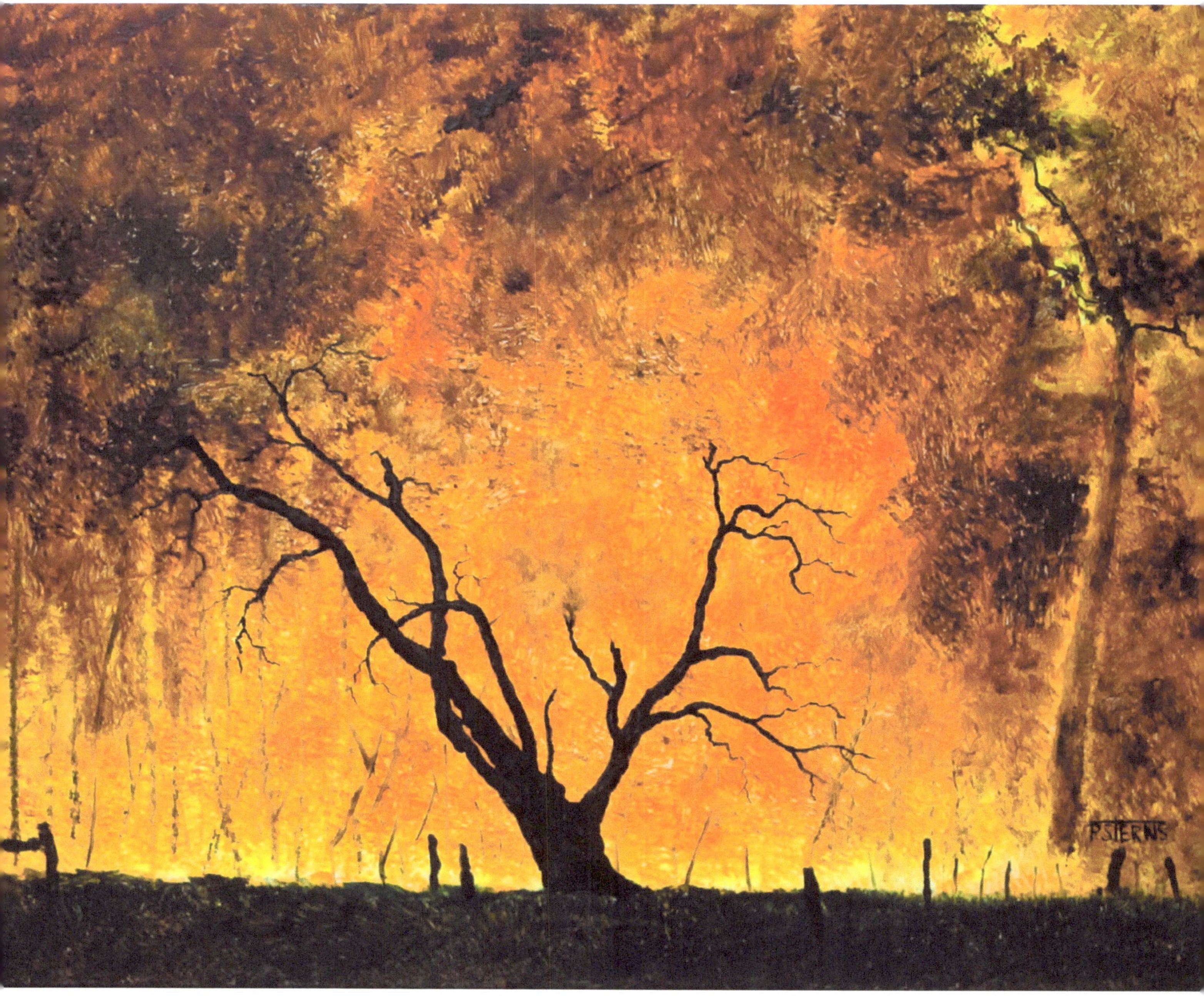
P.STERNS

The day

Well, here it is, it's Christmas day
The world has gone its separate way
For since the day that Christ was born
Humanity is split and now is torn
And we just live and no-one will pray

The difference

There are the rich and the poor
They live on a track or the avenue
Some drive a car with a fridge
They are known as the super-rich
But give a thought to those with none
Not through something they have done
There are some that now will say
We won't even have a Hobart racing day
Oh, how dreadful that must be
Compared to those that cannot see
These are the poor, the old, the sick
Measured with the rich man's stick
Many now have lost their job
That's tough luck, said the snob
Just don't you give me a call
A sympathetic Christmas to you all

The dragon's dream!

I have seen what the dragon dreams
As he dreams of the years gone by
They were all those golden dreams
Where are they now he wonders why
Knights so proud as they fought so brave
Are they gone with the autumn sun
Am I now in this timeless grave
Never more to see my home
Shining swords and battle cries
They are gone forever more
Aching heart forever lies
Here behind this rusted door
Dreams that lie on the floor
They are gone forever more!

The dream!

In this world I have been to places
They are never heard of, seldom seen
A little photo shows my family's faces
A lovely smile like a bright sun beam

And the other day as I lay dreaming
I cast my eyes across the sea
I saw a boat and it was sailing
To far of Ireland, to Galway Bay

The stars were shining on the water
There were tears running down my face
I was thinking of my wife and daughter
I left behind in that far away place

But then I heard it, a bit of laughter
What I saw was the sun and grass so green
There they were, my wife and daughter
And what I had was just a dream!

The echo of love

There are times when I recall her kisses
Others when my heart is as empty as the air
But most of all what my heart misses
Is the one that I called my lady fair
But she is gone now, it's been quite a while
And yet here memory just lingers on
That's when I see her eyes, her smile
And know that despite it all, love lives on
Time and distance are really nothing at all
Where the heart and love are concerned
As long as you know you can stand tall
That you lived, you loved and you learned
That no matter what the poets have said
And all that has passed and has been done
That whether you have lived or now are dead
The thing that mattered is that she was the one
So now I am learning no longer to cry
And stand on my own two feet like a man
Look at the past through my mind's eye
For the future is now, the past was then

The end of the line!

I just hope that I'm forgiven
When my journey one day ends
And before I stop living
I would want to make amends!

As I go up to the heavens
It's the Lord I wish to find
And I pray they keep on living
All the ones I left behind.

Let me see the great blue yonder
I am weary and I'm weak
Let me see the heavenly wonder
For it's redemption that I seek!

As I move way past tomorrow
Along the path of the setting sun
My heart is filled with sorrow
There was much more I could have done.

The final dream!

The stars are bright, the ends in sight
I have no other needs
You were my wife, you were my life
Full of love and splendid deeds.

I see the light, the gate above
It's peaceful now it seems
I feel the warmth, I feel the love
It's like floating down a stream.

So do not disturb, my dying dream
Do not shed your tears
I am now on God's new team
After all of ninety-seven years!

The final score

There is no measure of what you are worth
Of the good and the bad things you've done
In the time you were given on this earth
That's not until your life here is done

And then the scores are finally measured
They are written upon a dividing chart
That shows if you were bad or treasured
And now forgotten or live on in our heart

The final step!

Another friend has passed away
Gone are the days of old
When Father Time speaks to you
You do as you are told
And for the ones we leave behind
The sorrow breaks our heart
But for the one who passed away
It's always a brand new start
So celebrate that new beginning
May their journey turn out well
Think of them while you are singing
Till you too hear that final bell!

The forest pool!

Here by the water the
Sun breaks through the mist
I have this feeling as
If we all been blessed!
I hear the murmur
Of mountain streams
Far, far away from
All my foolish dreams!

The future

Years from now the day will come
When I find that illusive rainbow
And realise that the stars, the sun
Are nothing but a great magic show
So let me live, let me laugh, let me cry
Have dreams that might not come true
But as the years slowly pass on by
Let me always love and remember you

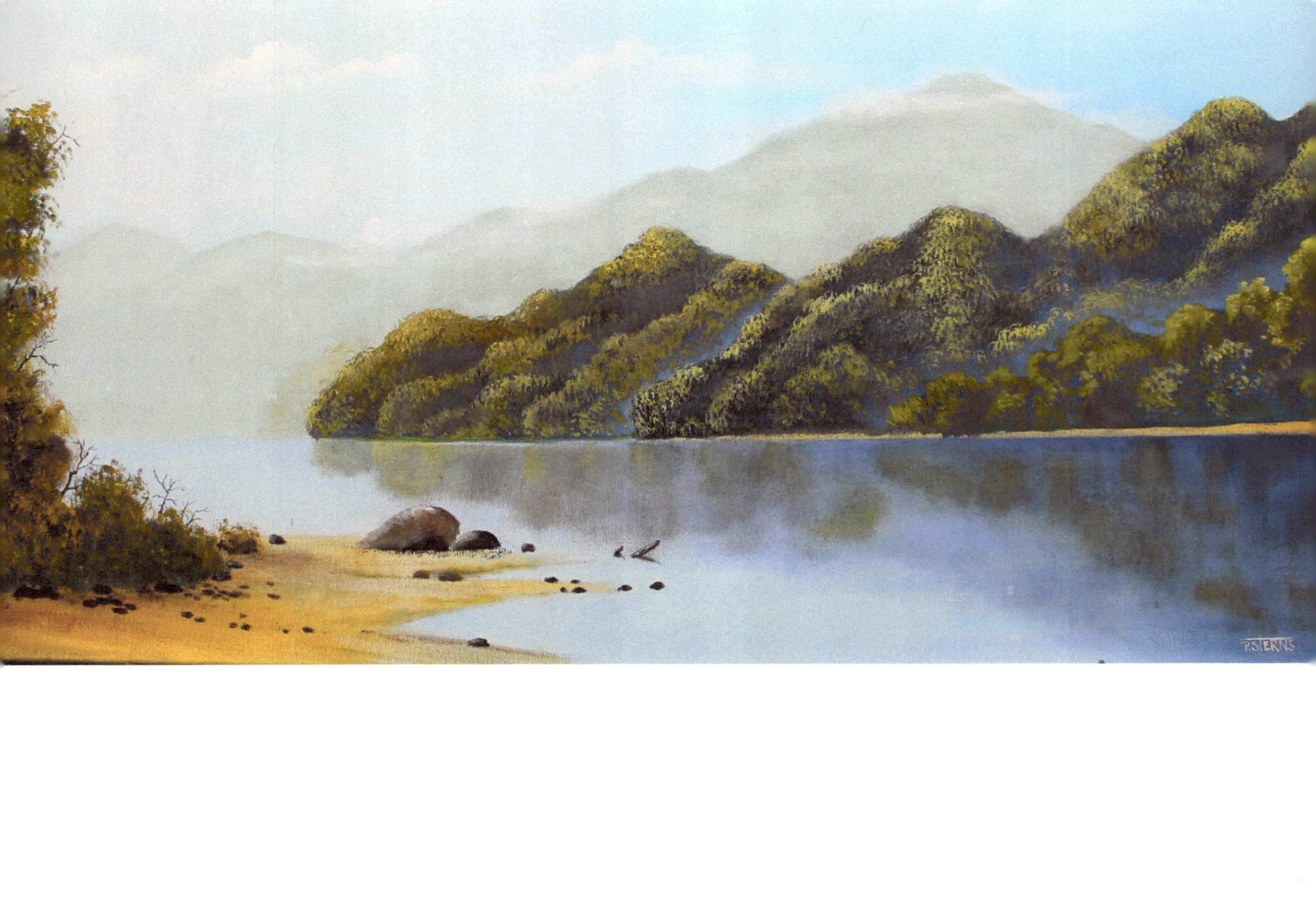
P. STERNS

The Ghan!

A railroad from Adelaide to Darwin? They have spoken of it for years
But to decide which gauge to use has taken truck loads of beers.
A lot of talk and through it all, the agony, headaches and pain
It was decided to continue with the old and trusted camel train.

From Adelaide the Alice on a train that was know as the "Ghan"
But to go on to Darwin had always been the final plan.
The Ghan started off just mere hundred and fifty years ago
And now that it's completed it gives me a wonderful glow.

Always wanted to travel to Darwin but thought if all else fails
I was prepared to accept that I would go on the Abalinga mail.
But I've been told that it's slow, so imagine this if you can
A boy of nine got on the "Mail" and got off a full grown man!

Now that it's finished I'm excited, because it's been a dream of mine
That when they announce the day it leaves, the platform and the time,
I'll be the first one on the train to Darwin, oh what a wonderful sight
Because believe it or not it was 1958 when I had paid for my ride!

The gift!

We honor our father and honor our mother
And sometimes we honor friends that we gather
Most of our live is determined by fate
Yet the friends we have are through choices we made.

So if you have more than one friend in your life
And that one is someone other than your wife
You'll know when you're old it's more than a gift
For friendship is proof that you have actually lived.

We often talk about crosses we seem to bear
But no one speaks of the friendships we share
Now when our life will come to its end
It's nice to know we had someone, who was our friend!

The good times

I never was a great thinker
Well, not according to my mum
But I was known as a little stinker
When I was still sucking on my thumb
Now the world has changed a little
And then again not really a lot
For again my bones are quite brittle
And once more I'm sitting on the pot
The things we once relied upon
Was milk from our mothers still
Now we just sit and moan
And swallow another green pill
Once we used to sing and dance
Until the early morning light
Now the shuffle makes us soil our pants
And a sneeze causes us a fright
A toupee is where the hair once was
And there's a stutter on our tongue
For our teeth are resting in a glass
Yes, the good times they are gone!

The hobo song

Fly me to Peru
Let me drink in smelly bars
Where people wear no shoes
And live in rusted out old cars
In other words a home like mine
In simple words – the sun don't shine

The journey

As I travel through life I don't see I just stare
I am riding a road that's not going anywhere
And I surely must be what they call blind
Can't see what's ahead or what I left behind
So remember to share, to love and to have friends
But do it real soon before your journey ends

The juice of the grape

Wine, wine, wine
Has its own sweet words to say
Time, time, time
It moves on and will not stay
But wine, wine, wine
It helps me through the day

The last man

I could never see the reason
Of why we hate and why we kill
Seems to me, there is no pleasing
Those that order it, can't get their fill
I think the world has gone insane
We go to church and we confess
Tomorrow it will still be the same
Perhaps more of what should be less
I do not wonder, nor do I care
Where the sands of time have gone
All I need is the why and the where
Do I go, now that I am left here alone

The lily pond!

I was travelling around
And this is as far as I got
There's peace in the valley
Where I found this spot!
The fish they are jumping
And the sun is going down
It's quiet, no one to see
We are far, far from town.
It feels like there's music
I'll sing along in my mind
Greetings to everyone
And peace to mankind!

The mystery

I heard the wind whisper a name
Don't know if it was yours or mine
And every day it sounds the same
Could it be I'm running out of time
What happens if the wind should go
Or if he calls out a different name
If autumn leaves are covered in snow
Will the words still sound the same
The mystery of the talking wind
Has been there since the word evolved
But man with has feeble mind
Has never the riddle solved

The old apple tree!

In the Garden of Eden stands an old apple tree
And he remembers the years that went by
He wishes the Lord would just let him be
So he could just forget, wither and die
It started when man was blind and couldn't see
The secret of life that Eve was meant to keep
About the fruit that grew on the apple tree
It would give us knowledge but also make us weep
But through the ages, through trouble and strife
People have come here, have loved and have bled
Referred to him as the tree that gave life
But all he can say is – I wish I was dead
He's weary of carrying the burden of yesterday's sins
Of the false pride of humans who always want wars
And who fight them even if nobody ever wins
And all of humanity that is now covered with scars
From the day that is known as the dawn of time
Till the Lord created the stars and moon beams
Showed us how to bake bread and how to brew wine
He has guarded the grave of all of man's dreams
So weary he is that he no longer can tell
Because time can play tricks with your mind
Was there a day when the apple really fell?
And is there such a thing known as mankind?

The one

Here I sit on my easy chair
Watching the world go by
And I think that life isn't fair
Time's got wings and learned to fly
I was in nappies, trying to walk
Eat soup out of a bowl with a spoon
Next I learned how to talk
Driving a car couldn't come too soon
Next I discovered there are pretty girls
And you strut, you huff and you puff
She's the one in this whole wide world
And what you found now is enough
But time keeps going, it is unfair
The one you once loved, she is gone
So now I sit in my easy chair
And my mind is still on the one

The paradox

There are times when I'm behind you
There are times when you're in front of me
There are times when I am blind
And there are times when I just can't see
I wish the answer was crystal clear
Not like a glass, clouded with fear
But because I'm dumb, I never heard
Anyone who ever spoke a single word

The puzzle

Is there someone beside me or maybe behind
Because I cannot hear nor can I see
Some say I'm deaf, dumb and blind
Whether in OZ or the land of the free
All walking to the beat of a different drum
It is much to the world's consternation
That we, with just one finger and a thumb
Have become the IPhone and IPad generation!

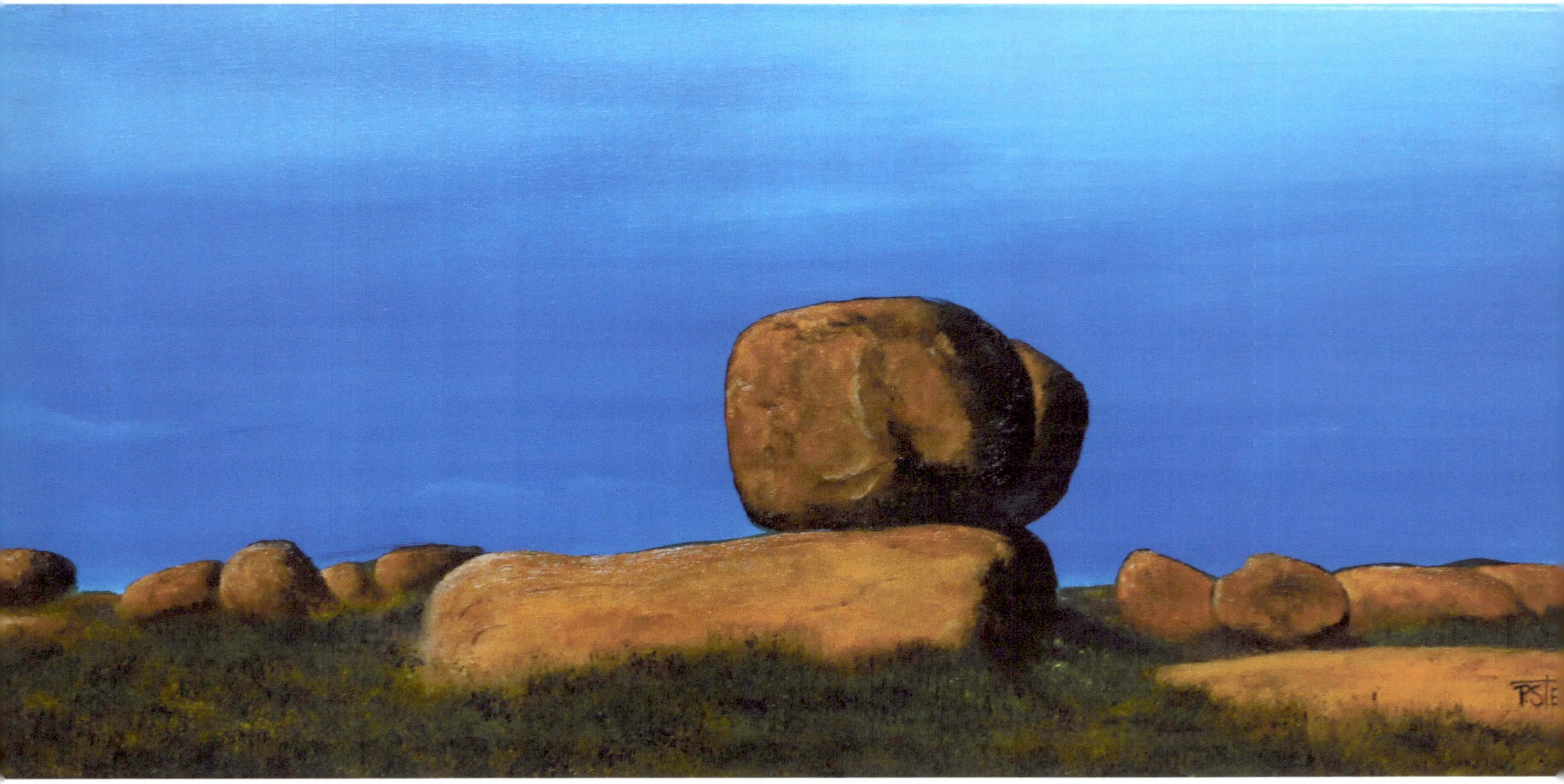

The question why

Why is it me Lord? Why is it so?
It's for us to ponder and the Lord to know!
Many have said – the Lord only knows!
Yet, when we believe, our faith only grows.

The question

I do not know what lies there yonder

I am not blind but I can't see

I cannot help but sometimes wonder

If I was there – who would I be?

The road of life

The road of life is hard and cold
With too many steps to mention
It's not paved with bricks of gold
But with all of man's best intentions.

The rose bush!

Don't pity me
It is my time
I have no feet
And I am blind
I cannot sing
I don't feel pain
But come the spring
I'll bloom again!

The search

Hey, pilgrim, tell me please
What you are looking for
Is it hidden in the mist
Or behind a secret door
The mystery cuts like a knife
But don't get into a rut
In case you pass through life
With eyes that are wide shut

The search

He's got no horse, he's got not cart
And years ago, he lost his heart
He don't know whence it went
Though many years he has spent
Looking for what he never found
Even when it was all around
Many a man will waste his youth
Searching for what he calls truth
But when the dust settled in his mind
He saw it all, no longer blind
Only to find that in his old age
The truth was there, yet he's no sage

The shadow on the wall

As I'm walking down the hall
I see the shadow of an angel on the wall
Could it be the returning of my love
Has she made the journey from above
Or was it just a passing dream
Cast by a lonesome sun beam
That was hoping just like me
To love again and to be free

The virus

People say that I fake it
Sneezing, coughing, all day long
I'm wondering if I'm going to make it
And will I be remembered in a song
I'm trying now to save myself
But the virus is taking its toll
All I see is an empty shelf
$2,000 for just one toilet roll
If toilet paper is the cure
For no medication can be seen
I tell now, and I am sure
I probably die here in quarantine
Two weeks in some forgotten hole
Not a single toilet roll in sight
God have mercy on my soul
Hope no-one else dies now of fright

The way it is

Tell me not the reason why
A teardrop glistens in your eye
The world cares not the circumstance
And life owes you no recompense

The window!

There are times in ones life
When you look into someone's eyes
And you feel you're cut with a knife
Yet others have warmth and seem wise
Some of them show nothing but lies
They are hard and distant and cold
It's no wonder then that we call our eyes
The window that shows us the soul!

The winner

Speak not of what has been done
Or of times long since gone
All the miles you'll need to walk
But now is the time to talk
Think of life as the rising sun
And you have won, yes, you have won

The word

Yesterday when I was out walking
The greenest of valleys I've seen
I could hear my Jesus talking
And the air was so pure and clean
There are those who hate His teachings
Or when He reaches out His hand
It's with love that He reaching
To all, even those that don't understand

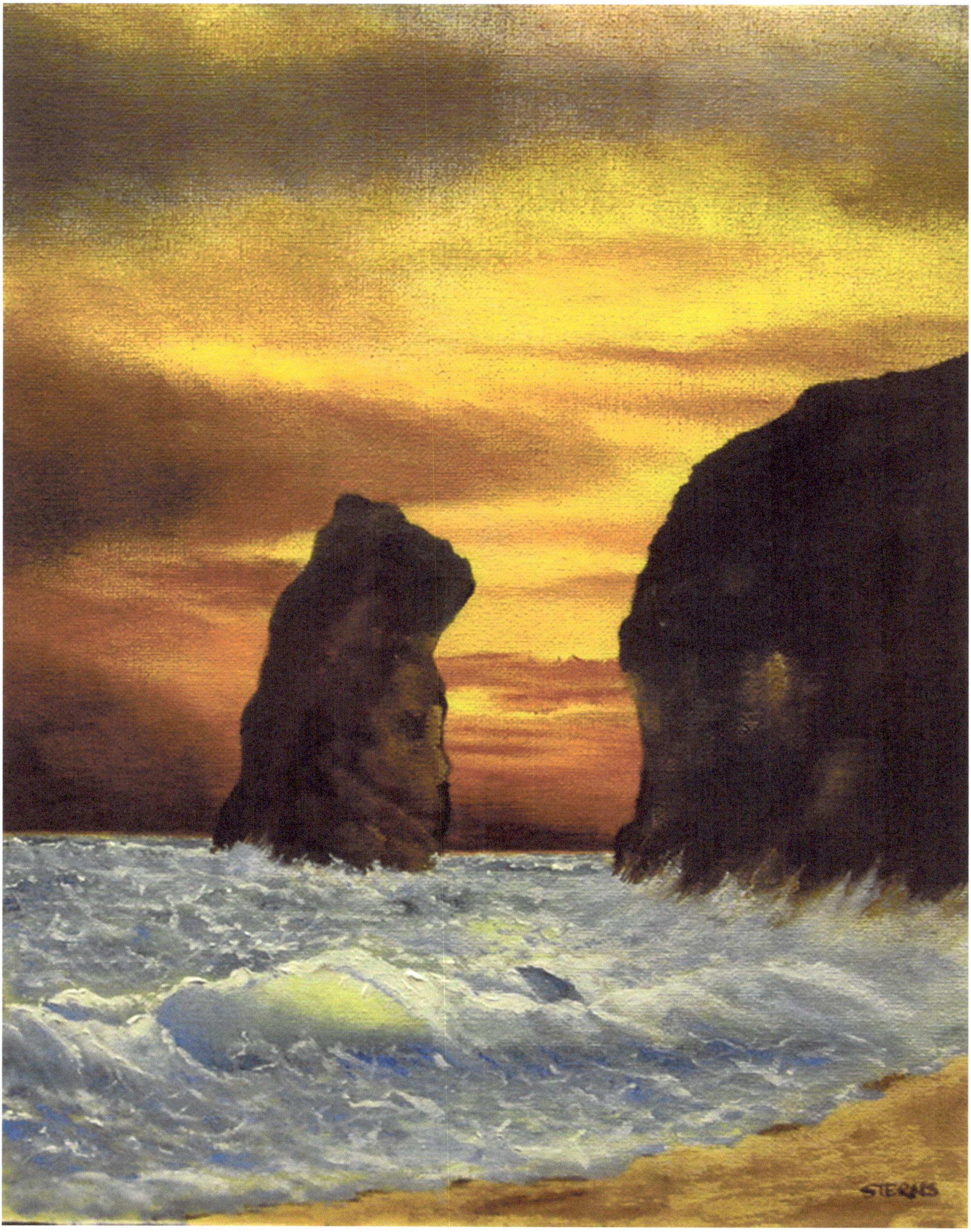
STERNS

I make a "nuisance" of myself.

The pain

Here we are, hello, hello,
as we answer calls to the radio.
Who is this, oh not again,
it is Pete, the phone-in pain.

He faxes us, and he phones,
always happy, never moans.
So of all the pains that exist,
Pete finally made No. 1 on our list!

Three words

Teach your children well
So they can spell
The words – I love you
So as the years go by
And you must die
They won't forget you

Ties!

On almost every other Sunday
We go to pray and confess
And tell ourselves that it is
Our job and money that bring us happiness
But if you are true to yourself
I am sure that you will find
That it is love and honor
Which are the ties that bind!

Today's prayer

Pray with me Jesus
Forgive the world its sins
For if you can't forgive us
There's no-one left that wins

Today's youth

They don't sing and they don't joke
Most of them drink and even snort coke
And they're seen with phone in hand
As they stagger across this land
But the thing that's really sad
Most of them just don't know where it's at

Travel plans

I'll travel from Paris to Senegal
See the beautiful city of St. Paul
I can do it in the summer or in fall
Don't know how I'll pay for it all
Guess I'll just rob Peter to pay Paul.

Travelling

It's said the road to heaven
Is a really long, long way
And at the age of ninety-seven
Seems to take forever and a day
I've travelled the road without a question
Every hill and every bend
And as a beer drinking Christian
I've finally reached the end

Undercover

Secrecy is what we need
In what we drink, what we eat
What we hate or what we enjoy
If our partner is a girl or a boy
Can't tell you who my friend might be
But his name is Syrup Tissues Lee

Visa cards

People tend to carry a heavy load
When they live beyond their means
They will travel down that lonesome road
Called the boulevard of broken dreams

Was it you

Who was the first one to sing a song
Who determined what is right or wrong
And was it day or was it at night
When someone said, they saw the light
Who decided what is old or what is new
Or when we are sad, that we are blue
And I never saw anyone who is weak
Hiding that so-called yellow streak
Who said that luck couldn't come too soon
And who saw anyone who was over the moon
What did they use to create their own luck
Who was responsible for it to come unstuck
Who knew the wise man that knew all will be well
I know he was born, but didn't come out of his shell
But perhaps they knew what was bound to go wrong
When they wrote the words to the very first song

Waste not!

In years gone by and that wasn't all that long ago
We had a device that was useful and thrilled me so
Something we take for granted now like the paper bag,
It is of course the can opener known as the zip top tag!

Now after opening to throw it away would be a great waste
And besides that, it would be in absolutely bad taste.
So I collected and sent them to Ireland, all other ideas it beat
I got a dollar each, as they made a perfect Leprechaun toilet seat.

The weather forecast

A little boy says with a frown,
the radio said, it will bucket down,
and the other thing I heard,
there is a small boat alert.

Dad, I better bring in all my toys
and tell all the other girls and boys.
But I wish it would just rain instead,
then the buckets couldn't hurt my head!

The wedding day

It is a feeling like red, sweet wine,
to know that you are going to be mine.
The feeling is so strong, so heady,
my hands are shaking, my steps unsteady.
All our hopes come true at last,
there is only future, there is no past.
The sun is shining, the sky is blue,
there is me and there is only you.
And there you are, lovely and pale,
in a white satin gown, behind a veil.
We say our vows, exchange our rings,
our love for each other, an undying thing.
Smiling people, they are all around,
we only see us, we hear no other sound.
They shake our hands, they wish us well
as our childhood stories, they start to tell.
We have a dance, we share a song,
and finally we are all alone.
Let's hope that we can always stay
as happy as we are, on our wedding day.

Weeds

My friend and I we both agree
Nothing in this life seems to be free
Especially as you get old
There's nothing like Mexican gold
If you can't get it when you pray
I guess you'll just have to pay
The cops they are so mean to me
They can't see things that I can see
They handcuff me, they got no class
It's a crime they say to smoke grass
They are right, yes indeed
But what's the big deal, it's just a weed!

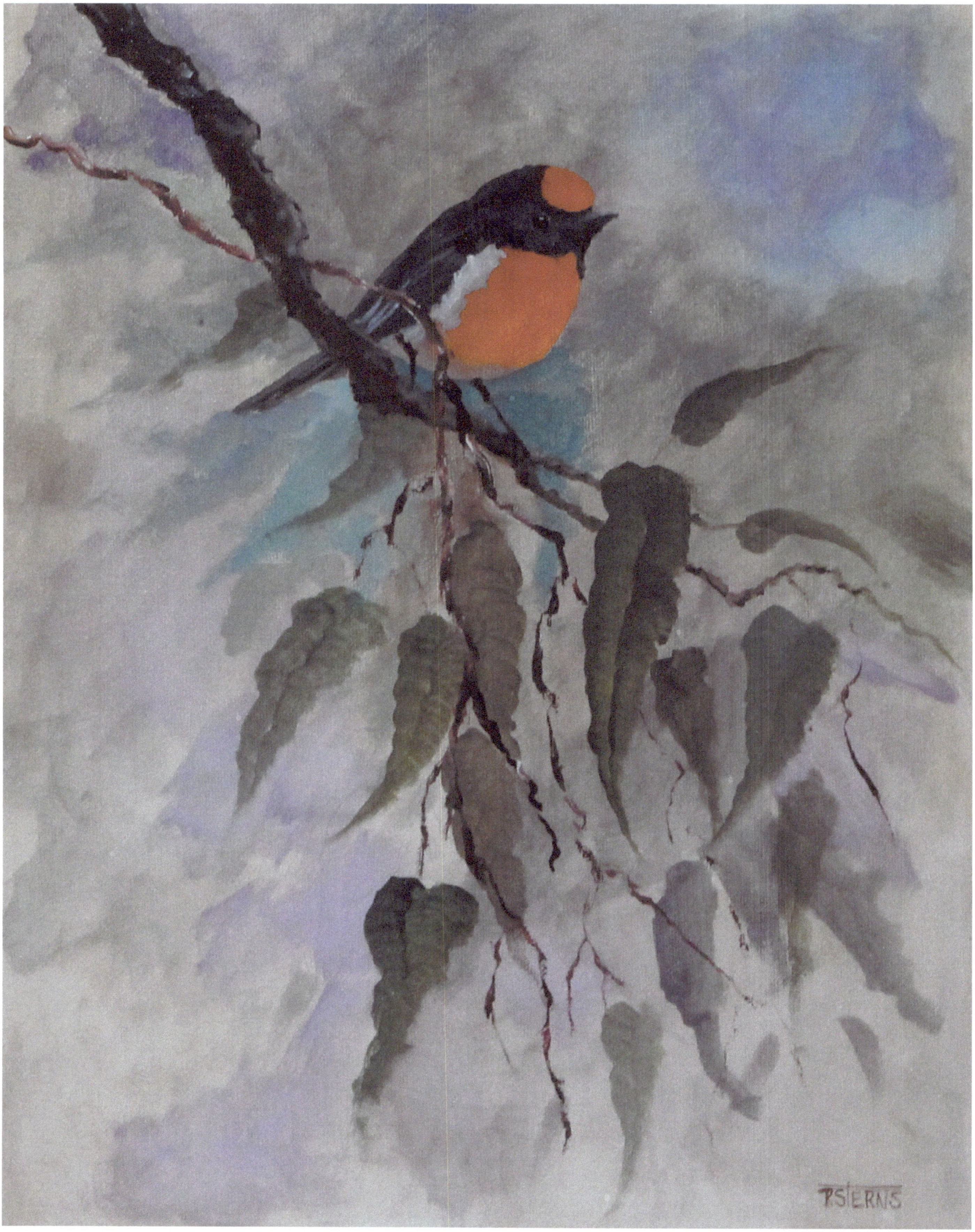
P.STERNS

What future!

Once I saw this ray of sunshine
In a sky so wide and blue
And I drank a cup of red wine
Sweet and pure like mountain dew
Summer wind and cloudless sky
All I could do is sit and stare
God forbid that I should die
With so much beauty everywhere
Yet there are those who sit and scheme
And it's not for silver or for gold
It is an age old hateful dream
The reason why cannot be told
How we fear this grey tomorrow
A future that is grim and dark
Is there more than pain and sorrow
Will we ever leave our mark
Will the memory we leave behind
Be ashes of the last green tree
Or will it show that all of mankind
Was one big happy family?

What if

If I was a millionaire
Would I be the boastful kind
Would I dance like Fred Astaire
Or drink till I am blind
Would I be kind and polite
Open doors for the old folks
And people from far and wide
Would they enjoy my little jokes
But I'm only a humble man
Who's sipping on life's cup
Wondering now and then
About life and just what's up

What if

Just one more coin into the wishing well
Twenty-six it seems were not enough
Because I heard old Johnny say
That's how he found his own sweet love
But can you believe what people say
It's called a wives tale I am told
They talk about it almost every day
They are people wise and old
But if it's true, I'm very keen
To change a molehill into a mountain
There was a movie that I have seen
Called – three coins in a fountain
But as there's no fountain around here
To throw in a coin or maybe two
I just have to wait and see
What a wishing well for me can do.

What is it

There is an answer that I'm searching for
But I don't know the question, you see
The same happened when I was twenty-four
And at eighty it still won't let me be
But now a question that pre-exists
Is how am I going to live and carry on
When this problem continues to persist
And nothing ever seems to get done
It's almost like the chicken and the egg
Which started, when the Big Bang burst
And if you say, you're pulling my leg
I'll tell you that I am dying of thirst
For my throat is parched and so dry
I've searched in front and behind
I'm sick of always wondering why
So I'm leaving it for others the question to find

What is love

There is a lot of empty space
Where once my heart used to be
Nothing there to take your place
Yet I don't feel footloose and free
You promised that you'd never leave me
That our love forever would last
Yet love can be like a forest tree
Not knowing the future nor the past
We speak of love and its afterglow
And we revel in its glory and might
But what do people really know
The wise man and the fool alike
We hear of the greatest love ever known
But if you really look you will find
What history itself has already shown
That love means you have lost your mind
Now you can search the whole world over
Till what you called love turns to hate
Call yourself a fighter, even a rover
In the end it's all left up to fate

What is real?

So many stories, so many lies
And yet there's no real regret
I'm flying as straight as any crow flies
It would seem that now I am dead
For where is the laughter I used to know
Where are the children that talk
And why am I flying here as a crow
Why not a human who's able to walk
Could it all be one nasty dream
Me flying here, just being a crow
Or is it because of somebody mean
Who's laughing his head off down there below
But if this is reality and I'm really a bird
Than what's wrong with flying and being free
It's probably the weirdest story you ever heard
But then again, you'll just have to wait and see!

What is real?

Those red marks on my arm
They are mosquito bites
And they never caused harm
Or ever started those fights
I seem to live in a twilight zone
Of what I think is a dream
I'm not sure if I hear a song
Or if I hear someone scream
The reality of the world today
Is a drug induced way of life?
The excuse that I hear them say
It's a reason to stay out of strife
I never had the need for all that
Life itself was enough to have fun
Waking up made me ever so glad
To see the stars, the moon and the sun
But if you feel that this is not enough
And you need to be ten feet tall
Then you never had a really good laugh
And you'll always live in a hole!

What is the answer

Eternity they say is such a very long time
No one ever said – that part over there is mine
The question's been asked a million times or more
Of people who are smart and seem to know the score
So tell me the answer, I don't care of if you talk or sing
But someone please tell me – how long is a piece of string?

What is the difference

I saw a bird up in a tree
Its feathers it did preen
And then, goodness me
A woman, playing a tambourine
The bird flies, but it's small
Can't speak but can be heard
A woman talks, is rather tall
Yet both are known as a bird

What lies ahead?

It has been a cold December
Christmas gone with all the fun
Ashes in the dying embers
Belie the gold in the setting sun
The roses that we loved in summer
Have withered now and died away
All we can hope is that someone
Will comfort us for another day
How can there be a new tomorrow
How can we live another day
The future looks so cold and hollow
For Father Time has had his say
The wrinkled brow, the shaking hand
No longer speak of springtime
The shifting waves here in the sand
Are bittersweet like age old wine
The memories are of a distant past
Remind us of how we got here
And knowing that they won't last
It is the future that we fear!

What matters!

There was a moment in time
When some things meant so much
Like making lots of money
And a kind woman's touch
But now that life is over
And at Heaven's gate I stand
I can see the earth below
And I come with an empty hand
Because it matters not a lot
If you are blue or green
The only thing that is counted
Is what kind of person you've been!

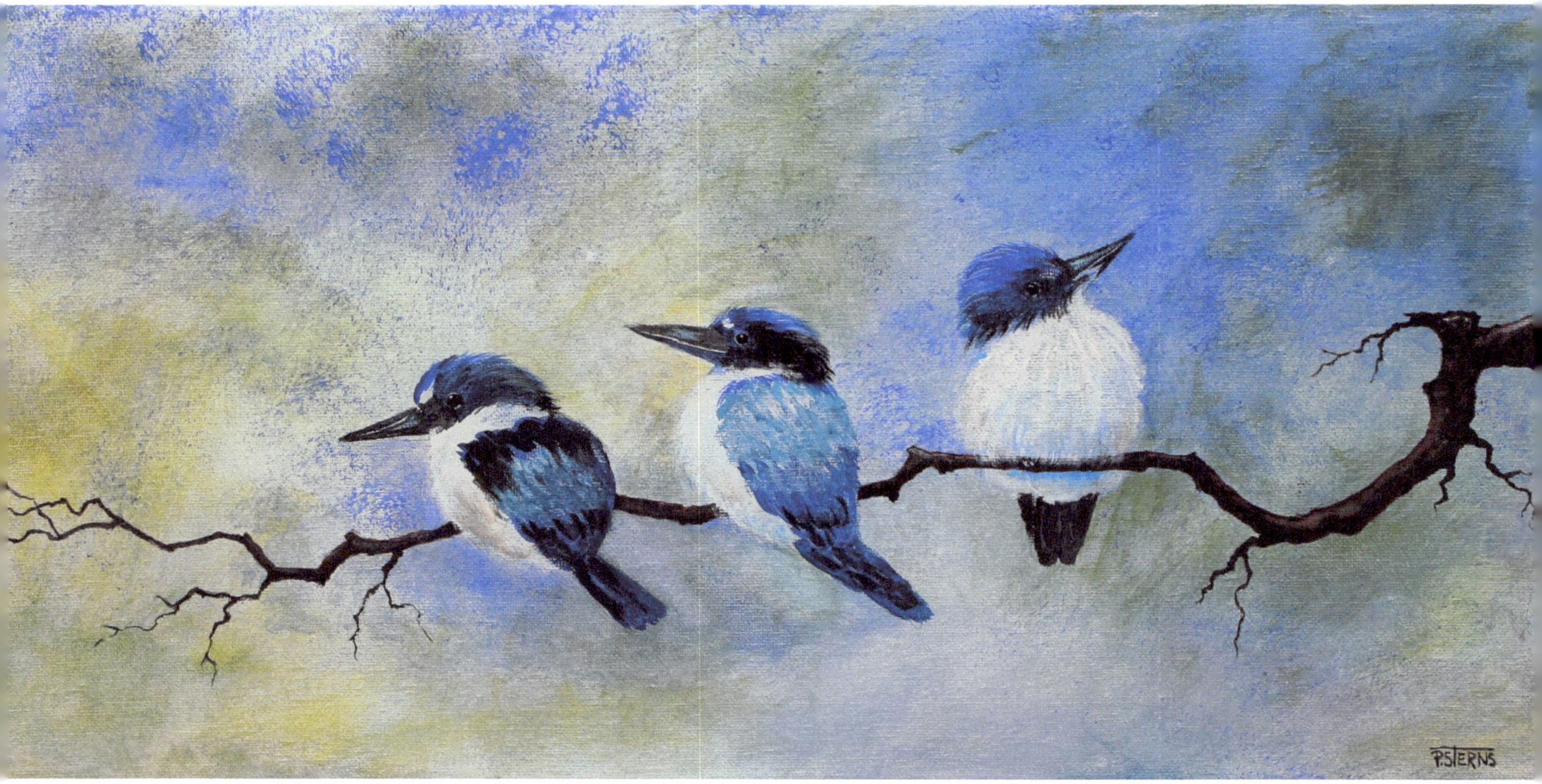
P.STERNS

Saw Val in hospital today, we are acquaintances, and there she was in a wheelchair.

I waved and she was so happy to see me, trying to talk and all I heard was a sound, a sound of someone who is happy to be recognised. Her son said she had a stroke some eight weeks ago and had her first little walk the other day. It was sad, yet I was happy to see that she is recovering and I hope to see her up and about soon, but I am sorry that I don't know her name.

What next?

Oh Lord, it is lonely up here
No one to talk to or nowhere to hide
All I can feel is this maddening fear
Gone are all reason and pride!
My brain says to go left
But my hand it goes right
I know I'm not deaf
But I can't seem to fight.
I know I am talking
Yet I see people stare
They hear me squawking
And I feel this despair.
The day it seems sunny
And I think it's a joke
But it isn't that funny
For I've had a stroke.

Ariel Sharon is critically ill.

What now?

Most people say that he is as hard as nails
Not willing to forgive or even to forget.
What will happen if his health really fails?
Will there be peace or a life of regret?
They say they pray for this man to survive
They say that they want him to live!
Who can say if it's the truth or if it's a lie?
If he does, what are they willing to give?

Some say that he's the salt of the earth
Yet others wish that he was already dead.
He says he defends the land of Christ's birth
And where once Moses his tribe had lead!
This conflict has been there for years not just hours
But they can't find a footprint where Jesus trod.
Can they find a solution before hatred devours
The people who claim to be the children of God?

What to do?

I see all those clouds above
And watched them through the years
As a river filled with love
Became an ocean filled with tears
Poets write about love so true
And singers sing their songs
Some so sweet and some so blue
How can they get it all so wrong?
They say that love is give and take
Others just don't seem to care
Some say they will take a break
To find themselves somewhere!
How do you know what's right or wrong
When life can be so unfair
Perhaps it's best to say – so long
If you find you no longer care!

When love dies!

Where does the sun go
When it sinks into the night
What is the gentle glow
That we know as harbor light
Why do I feel like screaming
When I'm sad and blue
Why do I keep on dreaming
When I think of you
Oh how we yearn for love
When we are in our teens
Than we pray to God above
For nothing else will work it seems
But than we come of age
And we think we know it all
We learn of hate and rage
And than our love will fall
And how can we forget
Things we say when we fight
The bitter feeling of regret
In the early morning light
Now my world is dark and grey
Over petty little lies
And it haunts me every day
When I could have been so wise
So where is the love, when it is gone
It's not like the sun when at night it sets
It cannot hide or be reborn
It's just memories filled with regrets!

When love has died

Via con dios my darling, my last song I'm singing
The love that we had, sad mem'ries is bringing
The years have flown, the love we had didn't last
And what we once shared, is long gone and past
Via con dios my love, let's not shed any more tears
The end that has come, has been waiting for years
What we thought was a love that was heavens send
Has run its course, it has died and come to the end
So via con dios my darling, the hour is late
Let's keep the good mem'ries and let's call it fate
Think of me now and then as I will think of you
Via con dios my love, it's so sad we are through
Via con dios my dream, this is the final song
We travel our different ways and I must move along
Think of me now and then as I will think of you
Via con dios my love, the sky no longer is blue.

When love is gone

When it's right it is right
And I do know when it's wrong
No use holding on to the hitching post
If the good times are all gone
What happened to the songs we sang
When we were young and so in love
That's when we always gave thanks
For the blessings from above
Now the times they are changing
There is no reason now or rhyme
I don't believe in what they call
Those healing hands of time
For who can tell what time will bring
Who knows the words to the next song
But I believe I know one thing
When good love is gone, it's gone!

When time is up

Once again the night is full of longing
Once again I find myself just so alone
My life had been so full of loving
But it all went with the sinking sun
And once again Father Time is here
Reminding me he was here before
As he whispers these words in my ear
That soon he'll knock on my door
But now my years have turned to gold
My love is still solid as a rock
When I'm Heaven's bound, into the fold
I'll say, I was waiting at the door for the knock
You might think I've lost my mind
For this surely means it's the end
But believe me, for you will find
I was waiting to take His hand

Where are you now

I carry the dreams of a forgotten time
When the sun and the moon shone every day
I was so happy, for I knew you were mine
And that was until, life took you away
So now all I do, is dream all day long
And at night all I see is your lovely face
There are moments when we sing our song
Come the morning, all is gone without a trace
I once had it all, but I now feel out of touch
For now that it has left, is all gone
I feel so alone, did I ask for too much
And I wonder each day, what have I done
I've looked for a sign, that you might come back
Never found a note about leaving or goodbye
So now I am travelling, that long lonesome track
Until the day comes when my soul learns to fly

Where did tomorrow go

Dancing here alone with a lonesome cloud
The music plays but it can't be heard
Millions of people that are called a crowd
They are moving but no-one says a word
But if you were still alive today
There would be so much for us to see
So many words that I want to say
What a wonderful world this would be

Which way up

We are old now, our hair is gray,
Still, there are things left we want to say.
I wonder as life this question poses,
Did we ever really smell the roses?
The grass is glistening with the dew,
Recalling friends that we once knew.
Moments that we keep in our heart
Where precious friends live and never part.
There are aches and there are pains
And for sure, I'll not be eighteen again.
As I see my neighbour do his chores,
Everyone prepares for a distant war.
My footsteps more and more are slowing
Yet I don't know where I am going.
But I don't care I really don't care.
And this frightening thought is always there.
I know one day I'll walk among those clouds,
Away from the hustle and the shouts.
But there is something wrong for that matter,
I can't find the lift, the stairs or a ladder.

Which way

I am a firm believer if there is nothing to be done
I shall give a helping hand just like everyone
I hate to be seen as a good for nothing by my friends
If it comes to decisions, you will find me on the fence

I hate the people who will never jump to it
But you will always see me have a go at it
With decisions so precise and ever so pure
Yesterday I couldn't make up my mind today I'm not so sure

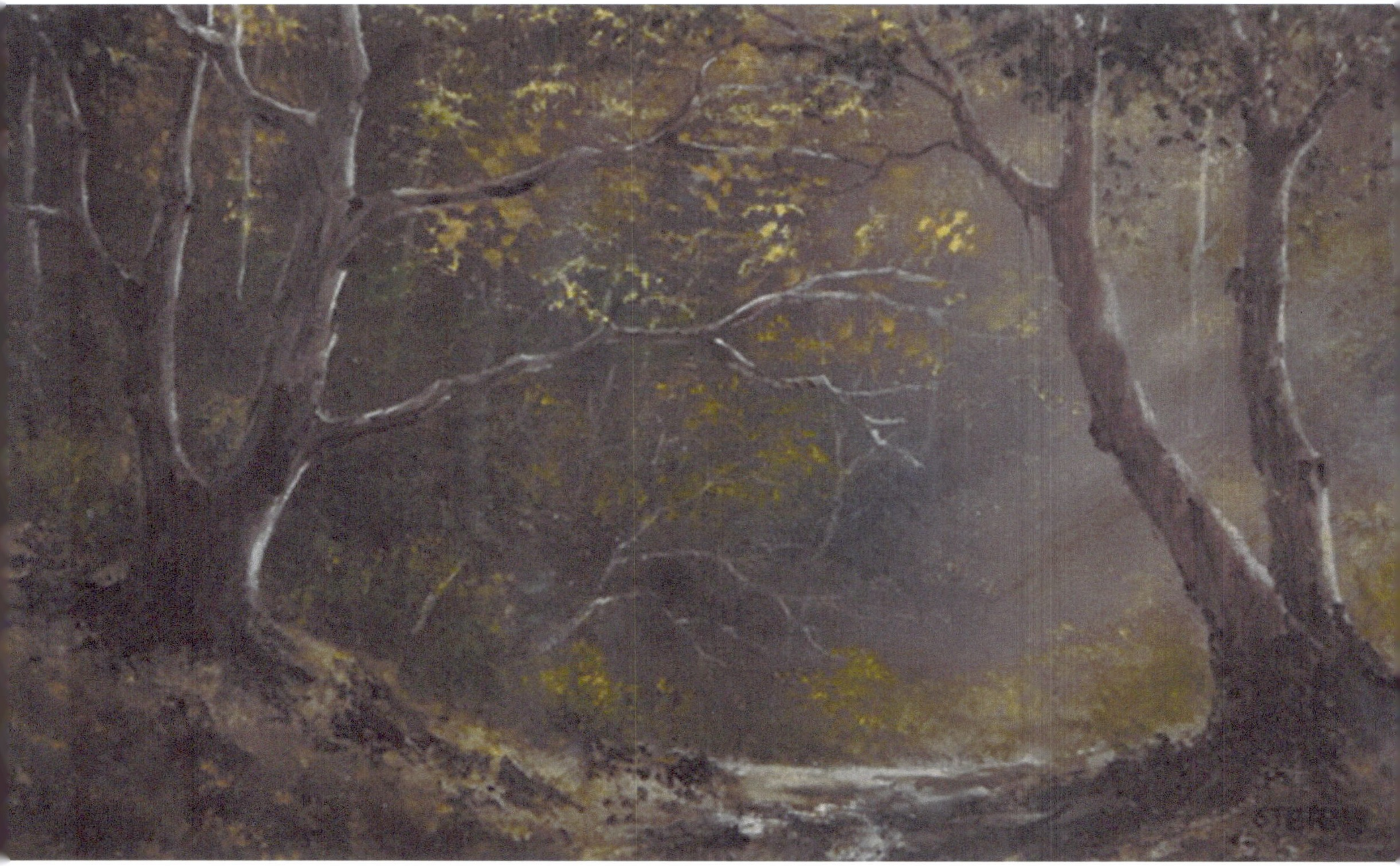

Whiskey dreams

I wish that you would talk to me
For I believe you know the score
Because no matter how I try
I keep coming back for more
Talk to me, I'm waiting for your call
You see I'm still the same old fool
That believes I'm 10 feet tall
Sitting on this lonesome stool
If courage comes in a whiskey glass
And wisdom in a children's rhyme
Then I believe I could pass
For I could be smarter this time
There is Peter and there is Paul
And they're dancing with Jim Beam
I wish I didn't see them all
So real in my whiskey dream
Your leaving caused me so much pain
There must be something I can do
I believe you could love me again
If I got off this here barroom stool.

Who am I?

On any day when I read the Word
I think – who am I to be loved by the Lord
The answer may never be found
Until I stand on that hallowed ground
When they call the roll from way down where
You can tell the Lord – I'll be there
And I know on the day that I'm gone
The Lord and Jesus will lead me home
I praise you, yes I praise you again and again
For you alone released me from my pain
And now that my journey has come to an end
Sweet Jesus, oh Jesus, please hold my hand.

Who cares?

An earthquake hits Haiti
The poor they moan and groan
The rich they throw a party
I guess life must go on
There are millions of people
Who do not know or care
How the rest of the world
Lives or how they fare
Tell me where's the justice?
When half the world is blind
And the rest of them practice
How to say – well, never mind
In a world that's super rich
We're hell bent on self destruction
And hearing – life's a bitch
But let's have more production
We may not live forever
For that would be eternity
And it wouldn't be too clever
If we couldn't live in luxury
You might think the rest of us
Are living on the brink
Yeah, well, what is the fuss?
Have a smoke and one more drink!

Who I am

You might think me charming
And that my manners are quaint
That my voice is disarming
And that I am a saint
But don't let that fool you
For I am not that wise
There are many things I can do
Yet I'm not a wolf in disguise
But if you should love me
I will do all that I can
To set your world and spirit free
And I'll always be your man!

Who is king?

When I was young, I thought I was insane
Everyone said – boy, you don't have a brain
But that was then, and this is now
I want to know, where did the madman go
Stand your ground and learn to do your thing
Hold your head up as if you were the king
Don't wear a frown, don't crease your brow
Remember they are all in your kingdom now!

Why

You can tell me you love me but don't say goodbye
Because if you do you will see a grown man that cries
I remember the good times that we used to share
Now my life is like a dead tree, broken and bare
My heart it is broken from believing all those lies
That love is forever and yet I still don't know why
We loved each other, were more than just friends
And all of a sudden that's how it all ends
Hopes and dreams they all vanish like smoke
Words left unspoken they leave me to choke
No reason, no rhyme and no words of goodbye
Still wondering, always wondering, wondering why

Why, why, why

What is it that a child might see
When it looks up to the sky
How tall will I be when I am three
And how old will I be when I die
Why is water falling from the clouds
And why do they call it rain
And why is a thunderclap so loud
And why does falling down cause pain
These seem just silly little things
Like a rainbow across the sky

No sound at all from butterfly wings
Yet the wind in trees will sigh
The world to a child is full of why's
Like colours in a kaleidoscope
And why does day follow a night
And why are we filled with hope
So never give up your wondering
Though they could be the childish kind
For someone might be answering
What you have been trying to find

Will you think of me?

Will you think of me
When years go by
Shed a tear or three
When the evening is neigh
Will the memories be sweet
Will a smile touch your lips
Will your feet tap a beat
Will you remember my kiss
But the years may go
And memories fade
Yet your cheeks might glow
When you sit up late
Will you think of me
And the love I gave
Will you think of me
Now that I'm in my grave
Let the headstone say
That my soul is free
While in this ground I lay
Still I only love thee!

Willy

Girls are made to love and kiss
And who am I to argue with this?
But if your are at the end of your time
All you have is love and very little time.
The reason why is what we ask?
Destined to perform another task?
I know we had our ups and downs
But through it all our love had grown.
Her life not easy, that is understood,
With too much motherly love for her own good,
Our children often made her heart bleed,
But always there in their hour of need.
She was a mother and a loving wife
With a lot of pain throughout her life.
Yet she could feel for others, the downtrodden,
You will be sadly missed – but never forgotten.

Wings

I wake up each day in the morning
It's another dreary old day
And I find that life is so boring
Working and all of the bills that I pay.
But sometimes I have these dreams
About a story that I once was told
And when I think back in time it seems
That I was just about 10 years old.
About a man who wanted to fly
Way up to the heavens, the sun
So I thought perhaps I could try
It seemed that it had to be fun.
For if I had the wings of an angel
I would fly up there in the sky
Not like Icarus, I'd know about danger
For I wasn't willing to die.
Then one day I made this choice
That at night I will close this door
And I follow this inner voice
And into the heavens I'd soar.
So when I fly up like a bird
And I'm sailing there in the sky
It's my soul that can be heard
Saying – I can fly, I CAN FLY – I can fly!

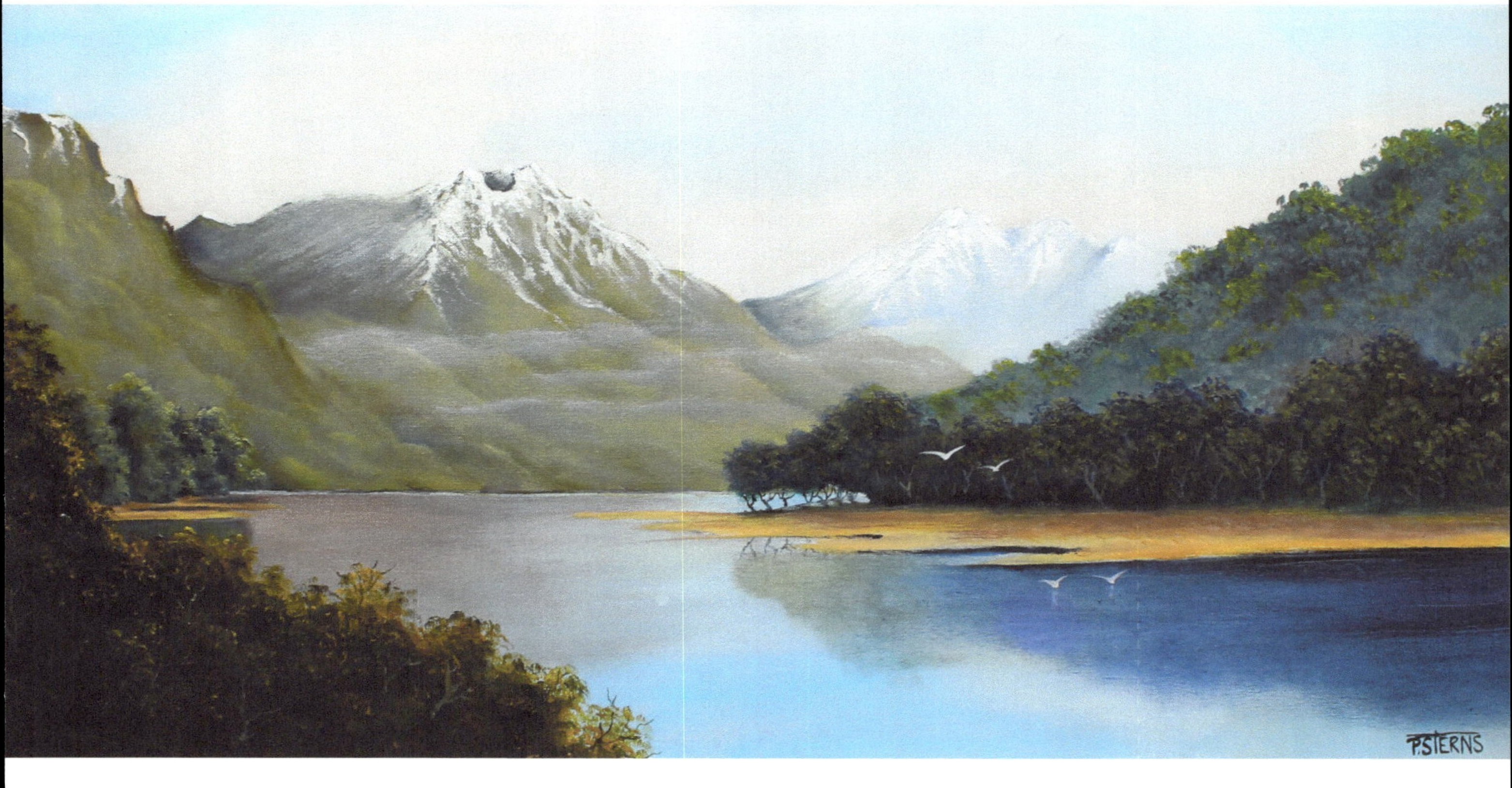
P.STERNS

The answer to roadrage.

Wishful thinking

There you are in the morning, happily driving along the way.
But then there he is the bastard who spoils your every day.
The sign on the road says 90 but 70 is all he will do
At first you feel sorry – perhaps that's all his car will do!
But now the road widens and you start to accelerate
You think you have a chance, guess what? You are too late.
Because he's doing 120 in what you thought was a bucket of rust
And he's leaving you behind, way behind, eating his dust.
As we get to the top of the hill we're back to a single lane
And suddenly this little rocket is only doing 70 again.
This has been going on for weeks and no matter how I try
If I leave late or early I simply can't get past this guy.
Road rage starts to develop, so I talk to the police
They tell me he is entitled to do that, if you please!
But wait a minute, I watched Coyote who's found his match
As day in, day out the Roadrunner he tries to catch.
So I watch the show, a name I am trying to find
Suddenly the word ACME springs to my tortured mind.
And instead of being angry and wanting to scream
I find myself sitting here as if I was in a dream.
Now I am reading this wondrous ACME do it yourself catalogue
And my mind is clearing from the angry self-destructive fog.
A disintigrator in the grill, a crosshair to line up this guy,
A gentle squeeze of the button, laugh like a maniac, feel happy, bye, bye.

Wishful

Quietly the sun sinks into the sea
It is time now to go to bed
It awakens visions of you and me
And words that we once have said
The Lord of All has given us peace
The moon and the stars now shine
The whole world it seems at ease
And so am I with this love of mine
But the world awakens again in the morn
And all is well, or so it seems
We can pray that with it, peace is reborn
And fulfil all of mankind's dreams

Wondering

Now and then I danced to Rock 'n Roll
There were times there was sadness in my soul
And then again I think of you and smile
That soothes my heart for a little while
But come the dawn again I'm by myself
Life goes on; there is no one, no help
It goes on, the only one was you
What is next, I do not have a clue
I know that once you were all mine
Gone are the footprints in the sands of time
Along with the warmth of the fading sun
And I wonder – where have they gone
Where have they gone

Wording

Someone said – I was rocked
Words that we speak every day
But I heard that Arty choked
On words he just couldn't say
They say he was up a tree
And totally at a loss
With words like sympathy
And especially with pathos
One day he got really vocal
And it seems it took his sanity
Trying to say equivocal
And found it was ambiguity
I'm glad he's not my brother
Or any kind of relation
Because one word or another
Is open to interpretation

Working man!

I heard it said that the rich man is busy dancing
While the poor man is working to pay for the band!
The farmer is ploughing fields and fencing
The government is collection taxes with both hands.
And the politician will be billing you
So someone tell me if you can:
For the days your work is killing you
Where is the pity for the working man?

World crisis

All the leaves are brown
And the sky is grey
FACEBOOK it is down
What a shocking day
Tried INSTAGRAM instead
It too was down, it died
Now my eyes are red
From all the tears I cried
MESSENGER was my only hope
It was my last chance
How is the world going to cope
If you see the Devil dance

Worries

I went to see my doctor just the other day
Told him that at times I'm feeling rather quaint
Asked him why my hair was starting to turn grey
And when talking to a woman, I'm feeling like a saint
My steps are slow and my sight is really poor
But there is more, I think, starting to divulge
I'm hoping for some tablets that will help me cure
What others, talking to me, call a midriff bulge
Without my hearing aid I just feel so out of touch
I got a shaking hand and I stutter when I speak
When I talk to people, I feel just like a grouch
I'm worried should I sneeze that I might spring a leak
He said – look here, dear chap, you are just getting old
And when he saw my face, he began to grin
I'm feeling so much better, now that I've been told
But asides from all that, I'm ok for the shape I'm in.

Worrying!

My friend one day said to me
How come you are so brave?
You stand there like an old oak tree
On a hill upon a big, dark cave
You don't worry that it might cave in
And cause you death or pain
I said – that is just the thing
Life is full of sunshine and some rain
If I worry what could be
I might as well be deaf or blind
No beauty of this world I'd see
Or hear the singing of the wind
There are some things that we can choose
And others that we can not
So whether we might win or lose
Life is simply our given lot.

Worth

How do you say goodbye to family and friends
When you find that your time has come?
Sometimes you feel the need for amends
For deeds and words that were wrong.
But you thought that with the passing of time
That perhaps they'll forgive and forget!
You learn to pretend that all is just fine
But in your heart there is always regret.
Written here on the tombstone of life
Are words for all of the world to see
Perhaps about a child, a husband or a wife
Or the last reminders of you or me.
So what is the life of a human worth?
Do we take down a cup and we measure?
Was it the good or bad done here on earth?
Or will it be the memories we treasure?

What are wrinkles?

You look in the mirror with a twinkle
as you discover yet another wrinkle.
You worry, frown and say :
"They are turning my hair grey,
and no matter how much I pray,
they just won't go away!"
So - you look in the mirror and smile,
WOW, that is a different style.
But now as in front of the mirror you hover,
to your great relief you discover,
that that NEW wrinkle you worried over for a while,
is simply the graveyard of your last smile.

Wrong direction

The duty of the world's nations
Is to prosper and pay their bills
But duty is a dirty word to mention
Most would rather shoot at will
Seems our leaders are out of touch
They refute that they ever heard
That duty and honour and such
They call them some foreign words
It seems that the thing they pursue
Are fame and public attention
That in itself is nothing new
Just don't forget your obligations

Years and years

A million years ago when I was young
The future was far away and yet so bright
And now it seems that all has gone
Yes, gone away, gone out of sight
But a million years was just yesterday
When I met you and fell in love
Yet yesterday wasn't meant to stay
And a million years were just not enough
What do I do now with a million more to go
I cannot cry and I can no longer laugh
My hair is slowly turning white as snow
I search for you, but are a million years enough

Yesterday

When my feeble life is all but done
And I am sitting in the setting sun,
Will anyone care from whence I came?
Or years from now remember my name?
At times it seems I must be dreaming
My troubled mind tries to find a meaning.
Did we stop here and there along the way
As we travelled along from day to day?
I remember things like a little kiss
Or an afternoon of stolen bliss.
And words like – yesterday when we were young
There were so many songs to be sung.
But I'm a different man these days,
Childhood memories shrouded now in haze.
And it's hard with life to keep in touch
But it's the little things that mean so much.
From what I remember, life's been kind
But it seems I'm slowly losing my mind.
So while I can and before I die,
I guess to yesterday I'll say goodbye.

You're not alone

I do not believe that the spirit will die
There is so much that we do not know
We humans have always been known to ask why
Only to find that we learn as we grow
I am certain that the years will pass
When I have died and my body is gone
But our love will go on and it will last
And although I'm not there, you're never alone.

You're the winner

I'm ready to die
I'm ready to leave
Don't sit and cry
Don't pretend to greave
The love I have
It is misunderstood

Put me in my grave
Between two planks of wood
So don't weep and cry
For I'm already gone
Just say goodbye
You have finally won!

Yule time

If I were to kiss you under the old mistletoe
I would be hearing a familiar ho, ho, ho
And that would mean it is Christmas, all jokes aside
The season of much love and a lot of foolish pride
But the seasons have changed as they often do
And now there's only me and no more you
But you are now just beyond that shine star
Which I know, isn't all that far
And as I wipe away another tear
Merry Christmas darling and a happier New Year